dedication

This book is dedicated to those who have allowed the truth to be revealed to me, at perfect times and in perfect ways, whether I liked it or not.

To my friend and colleague Christina Pirello, whose friendship, integrity, vision, dedication, strength, and insight is a continuous inspiration to me.

To brother Todd McCormick and all the others who pay an unconscionable tax for their love and respect for "mankind's most useful and safe plant."

And especially to Moonrose, without whom this book would not have been written.

acknowledgments

I extend my deepest gratitude and appreciation to Christina Pirello, Brigitte Mars, Katherine Dubsky, Deborah Jacobson, Pamela Austin, the International Hemp Association, and Bill Shurtleff.
Extra-special thanks to Robert C. Clarke for many of the drawings and photos used in this book.

The HempNut Cookbook

Richard Rose

Brigitte Mars

edited by Christina Pirello

Book Publishing Company
Summertown, Tennessee

Published in the United States by
Book Publishing Company
P.O. Box 99
Summertown, TN 38483
1-888-260-8458

Printed in Canada

ISBN 1-57067-142-7

09 08 07 06 05 04   6 5 4 3 2 1

Rose, Richard, 1956-
  The hempnut cookbook / Richard Rose, Brigitte Mars ; edited by Christina Pirello.—2nd ed.
    p. cm.
  Includes bibliographical references and index.
  ISBN 1-57067-142-7
  1. Cookery (Hemp). 2. Hemp. I. Mars, Brigitte. II. Pirello, Christina. III. Title.

TX814.5.H45R67 2004
641.6'353—dc22

MAY 2005

2004008732

This book is for educational and entertainment purposes only. Nothing in this book shall be construed as medical or legal advice. We recommend that you consult your physician before beginning any diet or for any condition requiring medical advice or diagnosis.

"HempNut," in all its spelling variations, is a brand name originally invented and popularized by Richard Rose for the product commonly and properly known as *shelled hempseed*. The brand is a trademark of Richard Rose and is a fully registered and used trademark in the State of California, the State of New York, and the Commonwealth of Canada. All rights reserved, worldwide. Material in this book may be used by written permission of the publisher and with proper attribution.

Please visit the Web site www.TheHempNut.com for more information.

Printed on recycled paper

The Book Publishing Co. is committed to preserving ancient forests and natural resources. We have elected to print this title on Enviro Smooth, which is 100% postconsumer recycled and processed chlorine free. As a result of our paper choice, we have saved the following natural resources:

BOOK
PUBLISHING
COMPANY

78 trees (40 feet in height)
22,750 gallons of water
13,325 kwh of electricity
195 pounds of air pollution

green
press
INITIATIVE

We are a member of Green Press Initiative. For more information about Green Press Initiative visit: www.greenpressinitiative.org

contents

Foreword

by Christina Pirello

The year was 1994. I was in my office, agonizing over the outline for my first cookbook (four books later, I still agonize), when the phone rang. I answered distractedly.

"Hey, Christina," said the warm voice on the line. I relaxed as I recognized the throaty greeting of my dear friend Richard Rose. "Will I see you at Expo?" He was referring to the Natural Products Expo (an annual showcase for natural foods) held in Baltimore.

"Of course! What's up?" I knew Richard to be ahead of his time, a truly innovative thinker with a penchant for the creative and slightly offbeat. I also knew that Richard had to be excited about something to be calling. We've been friends since the early 1980s, both of us pioneers in the tofu industry, always looking to the next horizon.

"Come by the booth—you'll see," he laughed. Of course, my curiosity piqued, I tried to coax information from him, but in the typical style of my friend, he wouldn't reveal a thing, except that I'd be surprised.

Fast-forward to the Natural Products Expo. Walking the show floor, I looked for Richard in the soy products section. Not there . . . hmmm. Looking through the program guide, I found nothing to give me a clue, so I walked the show looking for his signature luxurious, long blond hair. I soon found him, in the midst of a crowd at his booth. I had to work my way to the counter to see what was so intriguing to the delighted mob. I braced myself for the big surprise, only to see containers of tiny little seeds—hempseed, as it turned out. Hempseed? That was it? Surely, he was kidding.

I stood back and waited for the crowd to disperse enough for me to get Richard's attention. After our usual warm, embracing greeting, I drew back and shook my head. I will readily admit that I thought my dear friend had lost his mind. Aware of hemp and hempseed, I didn't think much about them, except from an environmental standpoint. I wished that our farmers could still cultivate this valuable crop, which yields fiber for cloth and paper, nourishes the soil, and requires little or no pesticides. I loved the fabric that came from hemp, especially its durability and soft texture. But food? Surely even Richard Rose couldn't pull off this one!

Over the next few years, Richard educated me about using hempseed and hemp oil as food, and I came to be a true believer that hempseed is indeed the hope of the future. My health and the health of my family has improved even more, thanks to the use of hempseed in our daily diet. Why? Hemp contains more than 30 percent complete protein, with all of the essential amino acids necessary for digestion. It is rich in the essential fatty acids omega-3 and omega-6 (occurring in optimal ratios for long-term health) along with respectable amounts of omega-9, trace minerals, vitamins, fiber, and other essential nutrients. Hempseed is a powerhouse of nutrition. Nutrients essential to the health of humanity and the planet exist in these tiny seeds and the oil pressed from them.

Of course using hempseed for food is not a new idea. It has been enjoyed throughout the world for thousands of years, staving off the hunger of hardworking peasants who ate it for strength and endurance, and as a component in traditional medicine. Still widely used in Asia and Europe, hempseed has been virtually off the radar screen in the United States, thanks to misunderstanding, politics, and special interest groups.

That is, until now. Richard Rose, always inventive, honest, and ahead of his time, has seen to that. His decades of trials, tribulations, and experience in pioneering soyfoods served him well as he developed the finest and most creative hempseed foods the market has seen—or ever will see, in my opinion.

Although considered the father of the modern hemp food industry, Richard never rests on his laurels. Working with hempseed and hempseed oil, Richard marketed premium shelled hempseed, even inventing the terminology in use today and developing breakthrough technology for better shelling and superior quality. He has produced the finest virgin hempseed oil, corn chips, veggie burgers, nut butter, and cookies—all free of THC and stunningly delicious. He even created a vegan lip balm that leaves your lips feeling like you've just been kissed—not just softly kissable, but as if you've actually been kissed.

And it hasn't stopped there. For the last year, Richard and I have been working together to develop the most revolutionary and innovative hempseed foods and products the world has seen. Our combined experience, wisdom, willingness to take risks, and the complete, mutual trust that comes with long friendship has formed the foundation for this latest adventure.

It has been my honor, delight, and privilege to call Richard my friend and business associate. When he asked me to edit the recipes in this important, informative book, and add a few of my own, I was thrilled to be involved. This book is the cornerstone of accurate information on hempseed, its rich history, and its past and present value to humanity. Richard's years of meticulous research and hard-won experience fill these pages.

Reading this book will lead you to the inevitable conclusion that humanity's future health rests squarely on these ancient seeds. To work with Richard, to share his excitement about hempseed, and to work with this incredible food source is continually challenging and inspiring. My experience with hempseed and oil has been one of delight and amazement as I discover recipe after recipe, use after use, for this remarkable plant's seeds and oil.

I may have laughed at my friend when he told me that hempseed was "the soybean of the new millennium" and the best hope for the future of our food supply, but I'm not laughing anymore—unless you count my giggles of delight in working with hempseed and the genius behind the modern innovation of its uses, Richard Rose. I hope you and your loved ones enjoy the recipes in this book as much as I have enjoyed editing them. Richard was right: Hemp is hope. How delicious for us!

Christina Pirello
   Host of *Christina Cooks*
Author of:
   Cooking the Whole Foods Way
   Cook Your Way to the Life You Want
   Glow: A Prescription for Radiant Health and Beauty
   Christina Cooks All Things Good and Healthy

Introduction

It's amazing how a simple vision, executed boldly, can change everything. If we stopped to comprehend for a moment the true enormousness of this particular vision, we would have to lie down and take a very long nap!

Instead, I ignored the obvious, rolled up my sleeves, and soon found myself up to my eyeballs in gô, the primal beginning of tofu and soymilk. But little did I know that God was actually protecting me from myself. You see, if He had revealed His real plan for me, I would have washed my hands of the whole damn thing and stuck to making music instead of tofu! After all, saving the planet by getting Americans to eat lower on the food chain was one thing, and making American-style foods from tofu was another, but making American-style foods from the seed of the cannabis hemp plant was almost incomprehensible!

The vision was simple: save the planet by changing the way America eats. As goes America, so goes the world. Eating less animal foods means less waste of water, earth, and land, and less pollution and deforestation. But how? How to change the way the world's biggest eaters eat? I could ask nicely, but it seems one of the birthrights of Americans is the right to eat whatever the hell they want. But what if I made it easy, like substituting delicious vegan foods for the all-American ones we grew up on?

Despite my being one of His foodie missionaries, saving the souls of carnivores everywhere, He waited fifteen years before laying out what had been the real plan all that time: reintroduction of mankind's oldest and most misunderstood food crop to America—the seed of the cannabis hemp plant. You see, hempseed hadn't had an advocate in a long time, not since the United States Department of Agriculture (USDA) literally begged farmers to grow it during World War II. Then, after the war, the feds couldn't dump the the noble seed fast enough.

It turns out that I was just the latest in a long and distinguished line of hempseed advocates: Washington, Jefferson, Adams, and the other founding fathers not only grew it but actually required the same of all farmers, under penalty of fine. Adam and Eve, Buddha, and Brigham Young ate it, as have millions of people around the globe and throughout history. Many were saved by it in times of famine. Asahikawa, Bangladesh, Canna, Hampshire, Hampton, Hemphill, and Hempstead are but a few places named for it. President Clinton signed an executive order protecting it as a strategic crop in time of war. Mr. Diesel used it to run his new engines, and microbiologists used it to nourish their bacteria. Religions and cultures around the world, in virtually every period in history, have grown hemp and used it for food, feed, fuel, and fiber. It's at least twice as old a crop as soybeans, although both hail from China. Every language has an ancient word for it.

But this time it was going to be used to make a cheese and a veggie burger. In America. In 1994. For sale in supermarkets and natural food stores in every town. Damn, I'm glad God snuck that vision in on me. Otherwise I likely would have thought it as loony an idea as I've ever had.

But it was too late. Once again, I was hooked. This way I had no chance to protest His clearly selecting the wrong guy to change the world, one bite at a time. The journey would take more than a million steps, but He was only letting me see the next three, so as to not overwhelm my heart and mind. Although I helped Americans to actually enjoy tofu, once known as "the most hated food in America," that would turn out to be a light prelude to the big enchilada: elevating hemp's status from the butt of every poorly written pot joke to mainstream use as an amazingly flavorful and highly nutritious food source.

Let's get something straight right here: hemp is the low-octane cousin to marijuana, incapable of producing euphoria but highly capable of eliciting ridiculous rhetoric, on both sides of the issue. Hemp contains no drugs and its use is not about "getting high." In fact, hemp is specifically exempted from drug laws and treaties around the world. Industrial hemp is not marijuana, and marijuana is not industrial hemp.

Shelled hempseed, the product of my great interest, is 9 percent omega-3 essential fatty acids and 31 percent complete and very efficient protein. It is higher in protein than meat or fish and higher in total essential fatty acids (EFAs) than even flaxseed or fish. It has no negative factors, except jail time if grown in the U.S. without a permit. Shelled hempseed tastes rich and savory, similar to pine nuts or sunflower seeds, and it can be enjoyed either raw or cooked.

Hemp is legally grown in many countries including Canada, England, Germany, France, Spain, Switzerland, Finland, former Soviet republics, China, Japan, and Australia. I'm convinced that hemp will be grown again in the U.S. as soon as there is enough demand for it. Then the right multinational agribusiness lobbyist will talk to the right politician and the right phone call will be made to the Drug Enforcement Administration (DEA) telling them to give back to the Department of Agriculture the regulation of the production of drug-free cannabis hemp, like it was until the last permit was issued in 1957.

Until then, I'll do my part to help restore the good name of hemp by creating demand for hempseed as an ingredient in foods and recipes and inspiring others to do the same. You can do your part by using hempseed in your cooking and demanding that your local stores carry hempseed foods of all kinds from all companies.

I've fed hempseed dinners to thousands of people from California to Washington, D.C. to Amsterdam. Hempseed tastes so naturally good it was unnaturally easy for me to make foods that everyone could enjoy.

Now my years of wondering why I'm doing this finally made sense. Although all my business advisers told me to avoid hempseed foods, luckily I listened to my heart and remained true to my vision. And now I have a fifty-yard-line seat in the creation of a new type of food, a new market segment, and a new industry. After watching the soyfoods industry grow in size from $75 million twenty years ago to over $1 billion today, I'm certain that hempseed foods have the ability to grow even larger, faster. Whereas in the eighties I tried, often in vain, to get people to just taste our soyfoods (even when they retained a squeamish scowl), today people are eager to taste hempseed foods. They even call their spouse over to try it, then take a sample home to their friends, all the while expressing amazement at its taste and nutrition and thanking us for our pioneering work. This difference in perception is key to consumer acceptance and convinces me that hempseed truly will become the "soybean of the twenty-first century."

Although my personal mission has not yet been accomplished, you hold in your hands the latest salvo in the campaign for nutritional food, educated cooks, and botanical justice. If the humble, drug-free hempseed can't get a fair shake in the Land of the Free and Home of the Brave, we will all be a little less for it.

I'm told I have a knack for being ten years ahead of my time. If so, then 2004 just might be the "Year of the Hempseed." So hempseed it is—but not just any ol' hempseed!

Richard Rose
Sebastopol, California

An early drawing of various aspects of Cannabis sativa L.
Photo: Harvard Botanical Museum.

Chapter 1

HempNut: Soybean of the Twenty-first Century

In 1994 I read Chris Conrad's book, *Hemp: Lifeline to the Future*. It was quite compelling, of course, but what really stuck in my mind was the part on hempseed's nutrition, especially its high protein content, which is about the same as soybeans. I realized that hempseed might be able to replace soy, with which I had made foods continuously since 1980. And then the copious essential fatty acid content made me sit up and really take notice: it was far higher than soybeans!

Now, don't get me wrong, I have nothing against the humble soybean. It's become the standard vegan (non-animal-based) protein source in the world, and it's low in cost and easy to grow. Soy is America's largest crop and millions are sustained by it. I've made literally thousands of tons of tofu by hand over the years from soy. And since I've been a vegetarian for thirty-four years and a vegan for twenty-four years, it has sustained me well for most of my life.

A soybean product, tofu, even inspired me to trade in my guitar for a curding paddle back in 1980 and radically change the course of my life from making people dance to making them healthy, a choice I wouldn't undo for a million dollars. And speaking of which, my persistent vision of a soy-healthy America eventually did earn me millions of dollars when I sold TofuRella, allowing me the choice between the luxury of early retirement or throwing it all into my newest vision, hempseed. So, against all reasoned advice, I rejected the lounge chair for a desk chair and began phase two of feeding the world, the hempseed way.

I decided to test my hunch and make some foods with hempseed. Back then, the only place to buy it was at feed stores, where it was sold for bird feed. Thousands of tons of whole hempseed were imported into the U.S. every year for birdseed, but not yet for human consumption. I knew we had to clean the seed well before using it. Straight from a foreign farm, it needed a good bath and a careful look for stones and the occasional nail.

Eventually, after eating one too many whole hempseeds and having to pick one too many shells out of my teeth, I thought what every bird undoubtedly must think as it picks apart a seed, "I want hempseed without a shell!" Thus began the genesis of what today is my development of shelled hempseed, the noble seed's first modification for the human palate in five thousand years.

But like most inventions worth having, achieving it was not easy. First, one of my staff spent many days meticulously taking the shells off hempseeds, one at a time. After a few days, we had enough to test for nutritional value. Hooray! We discovered that most of the nutrition is in the kernel, with the shell mainly composed of fiber, a little fat, and chlorophyll. Now I knew we really did have something worth pursuing further. We worked on how we could shell hempseed in large quantities, testing different rollers, presses, impacters, and disintegrators, as well as various methods of heat, cold, microwave, sprouting, popping, extrusion, and more. Although imperfect, impact shelling, which was developed in Germany, became the first technology for separating the shell from the kernel. Eventually I developed new technology, a technique to make the quantum leap from birdseed to a high-quality, nutraceutical vitamin supplement, resulting in better-shelled hempseed at a lower cost, with less loss, less breakage, fewer shell pieces, no bacteria, and no THC.

When we first started developing shelled hempseed, I invented the brand name "HempNut" for it. Like many first terms, it has become the shorthand name for shelled hempseed. Based on an ancient grain, our HempNut brand has inspired an entirely new segment of the food industry. It also has encouraged many people to start new hemp food companies to carry out their own vision of a hempseed future.

Now hempseed is out of the feed store and in the vitamin aisle. And that ancient, Chinese "royal grain" is entering its sixth millennium as a delicious and natural nutraceutical, ideal for improving the nutrition and flavor of any and every food.

Shelled hempseed, HempNut brand.
Photo: Larry Stanley

Chapter 2

Hempseed: 5,000 Years As Food

While conducting the research for this book, I was able to obtain many documents from around the world that shed light on the widespread and ancient history of hempseed. I uncovered many references to hempseed's extensive and uncommon uses. My research revealed that hemp's importance to mankind was much greater than previously known. I knew that documenting its incredible and virtually worldwide history as a food would be a critical first step toward achieving modern acceptance of hempseed.

Hemp is native to China, where we were able to document cultivation as early as five thousand years ago, and possibly as far back as twelve thousand years ago. The earliest Chinese references to hemp are in the *Ch'i Min Yao Shu*. Both the plant and cloth made from it are mentioned many times in classical texts, including the *Shih Ching* (eleventh century B.C.E.), *Chou Li*, and *Li Chi* (both about 100 to 200 B.C.E.). Imprints of hemp cloth have been identified on Neolithic pots from the site of Pan-pho in Shensi, China. Religious Shinto ceremonies in Japan still require the use of hempen ritual cloths, where the plant is specially grown on one "hemp island."

Not only has hemp fiber been used for thousands of years to make cloth, rope, and paper; hempseed also has been used just as long to make food and oil. In fact, it is one of the first cultivated crops in China. For comparison, the soybean *(Glycine Max)* has been around for only about three thousand years, and, like hempseed, also comes from China. In the sixth century A.D., the *Ch'i Min Yao Shu* advises: "Some of China's most important crops, like rice, millet, and hemp, have been cultivated since Neolithic times. . . . It seems probable that the earliest oil-crops cultivated in China were brassicas and hemp."

Hempseed was the sole source of edible vegetable oil in areas of Asia where imported vegetable oils were unavailable or prohibitively expensive. Locally grown hempseed and the hempseed oil pressed from it were observed by a National Geographic expedition documenting traditional Nepalese village life in the 1970s. Today, the consumption of raw or roasted hempseed is very common in China, and it has remained a popular traditional food for centuries. Noted hemp researcher Robert C. Clarke provided me with pictures and this exclusive account of hempseed tofu still made today in China:

Throughout China's long history, hemp was a much more important crop for both fiber and food than it is today. Han Chinese, as well as the minority nationalities, regularly made a nutritious, tofu-like curd from hempseed. Presently, only a few rural Chinese with strong cultural links to hemp continue to make hempseed curd. It is considered a rich, nutritious food and therefore used sparingly.

The following account is from a session with Miao/Hmong respondents within my study area who arranged for me to experience hempseed "tofu" production firsthand in March 2000.

Fennel greens added to hempseed curd by indigenous Chinese making hempseed "tofu."
Photo: Robert C. Clarke—International Hemp Association

Step 1: Hempseed is thoroughly washed with clean water before making curd. The wet hempseed is then ladled one scoop at a time into the mouth at the top of the stone mill.

Step 2: The coarsely ground, wet hempseed mash squeezes out from the side of the mill. The seeds are milled only once.

Step 3: When enough hempseed has been ground for one meal, the seed mash is scraped into a bucket at the end of a hollowed tree trunk. The mill is then rinsed with fresh water, and all of the seed mash and rinse water is collected together in the bucket. The pieces of seed shell sink to the bottom of the milky hempseed-water suspension.

Step 4: The seed mash and water mixture is poured into a rice sack and squeezed to collect the hempseed "milk" in the bucket. The hempseed "cake" left behind is fed to cattle.

Step 5: As the hemp milk simmers at a low boil, fennel greens are added to the mixture before it begins to curdle. The fennel greens taste great and hold the soft curd together. After about half an hour, the curds and fennel greens have floated to the top and are removed to the table to be consumed.

Step 6: The vegan, creamy hempseed curd is very tasty. If congealed more and drained, it would be a similar product to soybean tofu.

In Japan, warriors during the feudal age often used balls of ground hempseed and brown rice gluten to keep them strong during war. Hempseed still remains in the Japanese diet and can be found on tables of Asian restaurants around the world in forms such as *shichimi*, used for seasoning, and *asanomi*, a tofu burger with hempseed pressed into it. Tibetans use hempseed in a buttered tea.

South African Suto mothers wean their children with hempseed and bread or mealie pap. In India, hempseed has been pressed since ancient times to provide a table oil for flavoring food. It still is eaten by poor people, who consider it a tasteful and nutritious staple of their diet. They mix it with goosegrass to make bosa, or with wheat and rice or amaranth to make *mura*.

It has been suggested that the Hebrew word *Tzli'q* makes reference to a Jewish meal of roasted hempseed popular in medieval times and sold in European markets. The first part of the name simply means "roasted," and the final *Qoph*, an abbreviation of *q'aneh*, is the word for cannabis.

Hempseed was an abundant food of the rural poor in fifteenth-century Europe because of increased hemp production for fiber to supply colonial ships with hempen sails and rope. The raw material came from the traditional hemp cultivation zones in northeastern Europe, where hempseed was made into vegetable oil, hempseed meal, and a smooth paste similar to peanut butter.

In the Baltic nation of Latvia, hempseed is traditionally included in festival foods on St. John's Day. In Latvia and the Ukraine, a cannabis dish is served on Three Kings' Day. A soup made from hempseed, called *semientiatka*, is eaten ritually on Christmas Eve in Poland, Lithuania, Latvia, and Ukraine. Southern Slavs offered cannabis seed at weddings to ensure happiness and wealth (perhaps tossed instead of rice, as we did at my wedding in 1998). European old country peasants planted hempseed on saints' days. Eating hemp porridge, they were more resistant to disease than the nobility, who considered hemp a food of the lower classes. Monks were sustained by three meals a day of hempseed in the form of porridge, gruel, or soup. The Doukabours, a Christian vegetarian freedom sect living in western Canada since the early 1900s, apparently prepared hempseed paste for food when they were in Russia. In the New World, they resumed growing and using hemp for food and fiber before and after prohibition.

Hempseed has been a primary survival food during times of famine in China, Europe, and Australia. Near the end of World War II, hemp saved multitudes of starving people in northern China. General Counsel Ralph Loziers of the U.S. National Institute of Oilseed Production told a congressional committee in 1937:

> Hempseed . . . is used in all the Oriental nations and also in a part of Russia as food. It is grown in their fields and used as oatmeal. Millions of people every day are using hempseed in the Orient as food. They have been doing this for many generations, especially in periods of famine.

Chapter 3

Hempen Politics

Any plant with as many uses as hemp, and used for as long as hemp, will inevitably become entwined in politics. Used as currency, in industry, and for survival, farmers have long been forced to grow it and then forced not to grow it, whipsawed by the prevailing opinion at the time. It's been called both the savior of the human race and the work of the devil, depending on the agenda of the speaker.

In the founding days of the U.S., farmers could be fined if they did not cultivate hemp for sails, rope, paper, and clothing. They could pay their taxes in hemp as well. George Washington and Thomas Jefferson were among the most outspoken proponents of hemp during America's infancy.

In the nineteenth and twentieth centuries, many U.S. Department of Agriculture yearbooks were filled with reports on the increasingly significant hempseed and its fiber yield and use by state. In 1848, the U.S. produced thirty thousand tons of hemp fiber. During World War II, the U.S. government virtually begged farmers to grow hemp to supply the military

One of the earliest Western illustrations of cannabis, from the works of Dioscorides (1st century). Courtesy of Robert C. Clarke— International Hemp Association

with critically-needed fiber, including the parachute rigging that helped spare the life of young George H.W. Bush when he was shot down over the Pacific (yes, President Bush's life was saved by hemp!). A government-produced film, called *Hemp for Victory*, detailed hemp's history and cultivation methods and its strategic importance to America. Copies of the film are still widely available.

Today, the U.S. has more than five hundred thousand acres of wild hemp growing every year, second in acreage only to China. Inexplicably, some of this drug-free, industrial, wild "ditch weed," a favorite of passing birds and therefore bird hunters, accounts for over 95 percent of the Drug Enforcement Administration's "marijuana" seizures.

Industrial hemp stalk, fiber, sterilized seed, and products made from them are completely legal under U.S. federal and state law, as long as they do not contain THC, the drug found in marijuana (also known as high-THC cannabis, whereas hemp is known as low-THC cannabis). These hemp products are expressly and specifically exempted from the U.S. Controlled Substances Act, as well as the international treaty on drugs. Prohibition of hemp products per se by the U.S. would be illegal, as it would clearly violate NAFTA and WTO rules and could be overturned by an international court. The government instead concentrates its attention on the drug found in marijuana, THC, which is restricted.

Since industrial hemp is a tailor-made Republican issue (states' rights, farmers' rights, farm aid, over-reaching federal government, pro-business, no drug issues, world competitiveness), the DEA may have sensed a change in the political climate with the incoming Bush administration. In October 2001, the DEA formally announced the legalization of an estimated 95 percent of all hemp products by declaring that hemp products not for human consumption could be imported even if they contained THC. This is important, because previously if an otherwise legal hemp product contained any measurable trace amount of THC, it could be seized as a controlled substance and all the parties involved would have serious trouble with the U.S. Customs. Since by law all hemp must be grown outside of America, all hemp products must be imported, so U.S. Customs is the first U.S. agency to inspect a hemp product. (See 21 CFR 1308 for details.)

Properly made hemp products for human consumption (hempseed and hempseed oil) are free of THC, so they too are exempt from U.S. and state drug laws, thanks to the DEA's new rule permitting the free trade of hemp. Still, to grow hemp in the U.S., a farmer must obtain a permit from the DEA. However, the last hemp company to get such a permit was in Wisconsin in 1957. While U.S. farmers clamor to be allowed to grow it, hemp is cultivated in almost every industrialized country except the U.S., which has to import millions of pounds every year. Around the world, sterilized hempseed and hemp fiber are legal.

More than sixty years ago, *Popular Science* stated that hemp had twenty-five thousand uses, and there are many more today. All around the world, fibrous hemp stalks are made into textiles and clothes for companies such as Armani and Patagonia, spun into twine and rope for the mining industry, and converted into carpets for Interface. The fiber is made into paper for Crane and Co., animal bedding, particle board, linoleum, plastic for BMW and Mercedes-Benz cars, fuel, and building materials. More than one thousand houses have been built in Europe using mineralized hemp stalk and water.

Hempseed oil is used in several popular products made by The Body Shop, accounting for 12 percent of sales after only eighteen months on the market. Hempseed meal is used in beer brewing in the U.S. to add flavor and body. In Germany, hempseed meal and shelled hempseed are sold to bakeries, where they are used like sesame seeds.

Experts believe hempseed will eventually become more valuable for human and industrial uses than hemp fiber. It is certainly one of the most nutritious foods on earth, containing all the essential fatty acids and essential amino acids needed to maintain good health. Forty percent more nutritious than whole hempseed (hempseed with the shell on), shelled hempseed consists of 31 percent high-quality, easily digestible protein, 36 percent essential fatty acids (the "good fat"), and 6 percent fiber. It also is high in vitamins and important minerals. Tasting similar to pine nuts and sunflower seeds, it can be used in almost any recipe. Shelled hempseed typically requires no heat or radiation sterilization and contains no detectable THC.

Hempseed has been a staple of the diet sold in markets throughout China for thousands of years. Photo: Robert C. Clarke— International Hemp Association

Chapter 4

A Protein Powerhouse

Shelled hempseed, with its high content of essential amino acids (protein) and essential fatty acids (omega-3 and omega-6), is the most nutritious plant food on earth in terms of its ability to sustain life. The total amount of nutrients deemed "essential" is almost two-thirds of the entire hempseed! Does any other food have such a density of nutrition? After twenty-four years of searching on a personal quest, from dairy products to raw foods to soyfoods, I have yet to find it.

Higher in protein than meat, fish, or eggs, shelled hempseed has all eight essential amino acids, including high amounts of cysteine and methionine, which are sulfur-containing amino acids often lacking in a vegetarian diet. Hempseed also is high in glutamic acid, an amino acid precursor to a neurotransmitter that alleviates stress. In addition, the quality of the protein itself is very high since it is composed of albumin and edestin proteins, which are globular in shape, similar to those found in blood and egg whites, and therefore easier to assimilate. Only found in hempseed, edestin aids digestion and is nearly phosphorus-free, which is important for kidney ailments. Highly-digestible albumin is a major source of free radical scavengers and is the industry standard for protein quality evaluation.

Hempseed is free of the trypsin inhibitors and oligosaccharides found in soybeans, which impair protein absorption and cause digestive problems, respectively. A significant number of people are allergic to soy products, whereas hempseed is rarely, if ever, allergenic. Furthermore, soybeans are now being genetically modified, which is not the case with hempseed.

The importance of hempseed protein throughout history has been well documented. In 1881 a German scientist first discovered that hempseed contains edestin, its main protein. In the early twentieth century, edestin was one of the most studied proteins in both science and industry. In 1915 the *Journal of Biological Chemistry* discussed edestin at length, presenting ideas that would later form the

PROTEIN CONTENT COMPARISON OF VARIOUS FOODS	
Soybean	35.0%
HempNut™	31.0%
Hamburger beef	27.1%
Fish, blue	26.0%
Cheese, cheddar	23.5%
Chicken	23.5%
Whole hempseed	23.0%
Almond	18.3%
Wheat flour	13.3%
Egg	12.0%
Tofu	8.0%
Rice	7.5%
Milk, skim	3.7%

basis for protein complementarity and combining, a popular concept among vegetarians. A later issue published a vegetable protein study; edestin was considered suitable as a sole protein source for animals: "Protein feeding in the future will be based rather on the amino acid makeup than on the results of past feeding experiments." The study also stated that "the relatively large amount of lysine present in the . . . hempseed . . . is especially noteworthy."

In 1932, a patent was issued for a gluing process using hempseed protein; today, milk protein is used in adhesives. In 1937, the same scientists who first spun vegetable protein for food issued a patent using hempseed protein to make spun filaments, films, and threads that are similar to silk and wool.

	HempNut™	Egg whites	Tofu, regular	Human milk	Cow's milk (whole)
Leucine	18.80	9.50	5.9	2.78	3.44
Lysine	9.10	6.48	5.7	3.12	2.72
Threonine	10.30	4.77	3.7	0.62	1.61
Phen+tyro	21.90	6.89	4.8	1.21	1.70
Valine	14.20	8.42	4.3	1.39	2.40
Meth+cyst	9.60	4.20	1.0	0.65	0.86
Isoleucine	11.40	6.98	4.1	0.75	2.23
Tryptophan	3.90	1.64	1.2	0.23	0.49

ESSENTIAL AMINO ACID COMPARISON OF HEMPNUT™, EGG WHITES, TOFU, HUMAN MILK, AND COW'S MILK IN MG/G

The nature of enzymes became known in 1909 when a British scientist discovered the protein enzyme protease in hempseed, which he called "vegetable trypsin." Today, enzymes are indispensable to the food ingredient industry and are used to make many foods, from cheese to flavorings to sweeteners.

Popular high-protein diets that are high in animal protein and low in fiber and EFAs should not be used for more than three months, since they can be difficult to digest and hard on the kidneys. Besides, they are not vegetarian-friendly and contribute to the overproduction of environmentally damaging foods that are as hard on the planet as they are the body. A balanced diet including hempseed is healthy, satisfying, and sustainable. Furthermore, less overall food consumption results in less work for the body.

Shelled hempseed was
first introduced to the
U.S. in 1998.
Photo: Larry Stanley

A powdered protein drink mix from Germany.

Chapter 5

Hempseed's Halo: The "Alpha and Omega" of Essential Fatty Acids

Hempseed is not only an incredible source of protein; it also has an exceptionally high content of polyunsaturated fatty acids. At 80 percent, hempseed oil is one of the richest sources of polyunsaturated fatty acids, specifically the two essential fatty acids (EFAs) linoleic acid, an omega-6 fatty acid (abbreviated "LA," chemical name 18:2w6), and alpha-linolenic acid, an omega-3 fatty acid (abbreviated "LNA" or "ALA," chemical name 18:3w3).

The body converts omega-3 to docosahexaenoic acid (DHA) and eicosapentaenoic acid (EPA), the two most critically needed EFAs. Omega-6 is converted to arachidonic acid (AA), too much of which can cause health problems. Omega-6 and omega-3 are not interchangeable; we must consume them both, but in the proper balance.

It's estimated that 80 percent of Americans have a diet deficient in essential fatty acids. EFAs are considered "good" fat; they are important to all tissues in the body and are necessary for all biochemical processes. Essential fatty acids are called "essential" because the human body cannot make them. The only way we can get them is through our food.

Did you know that the brain is 12 percent fat, mother's milk is 40 percent fat, and the eyes are 60 percent fat, of which DHA from omega-3 is the most abundant? DHA stays in the body for about one week, so a daily supply is not necessary. Besides omega-3, DHA is found in fish and in the source from which the fish obtain it: microalgae wild in the sea, or cultured microalgae in DHA factories.

Hempseed oil contains approximately 60 percent omega-6 and 20 percent omega-3. Shelled hempseed consists of about 27 percent omega-6 and 9 percent omega-3, much more than any fish, meat, or other food except flaxseed. Remember hearing that fish is "brain food"? Well, if this is true, shelled hempseed is "super brain food," since it's significantly higher in omega-3 than fish. The Chinese have long called fish a food for a "balanced, happy mood and better mental performance." A wide range of clinical studies conducted during the past thirty years have shown that omega-3 fatty acids are important for many bodily functions and are necessary for our survival.

Some suggest that Homo sapiens' survival over Neanderthal man was due to our species' consumption of fish rich in EFAs, while the Neanderthal ate red meat low in EFAs. Others suggest that cannabis was the first reason for people to stay in one place and become farmers, rejecting a nomadic life without cannabis. Certainly if the human species was equipped with just one plant for its survival, cannabis would be the right one, considering its many diverse and important uses.

EFAs have a slippery quality that help make blood platelets less sticky. Sticky platelets clot more easily and can block blood vessels, causing stroke, heart attack, and embolisms.

The 3:1 ratio of omega-6 to omega-3 in hempseed is optimal for long-term health maintenance, as it is the same ratio found in healthy human tissue. This ratio is unique among plant oils. Flaxseed (linseed) oil, another rich source of EFAs, has the opposite ratio, or 1:3. Therefore, flaxseed oil is superior for short-term treatment of omega-3 deficiency, but it is unsuitable as a long-term dietary staple since it is omega-3 heavy. Hempseed oil, however, is better for long-term health maintenance because of its proper EFA balance.

Although there is no official recommended daily allowance for EFAs, many experts have made recommendations. They advise consuming a minimum of 3 percent of calories from omega-6 and 1 percent from omega-3 fatty acids. Pregnant or lactating women should double their intake of omega-3 to 2 percent of calories, due to the critical importance of omega-3 for the developing fetus. The average adult consumes about 2,000 calories per day—2,500 if active or athletic. Assuming there is no EFA deficiency to compensate, the average adult needs 3 percent of 2,000 calories of omega-6 and 1 percent of 2,000 calories of omega-3. That computes to 6.6 grams of omega-6 and 2.2 grams of omega-3 per day (fats supply 9 calories per gram).

Omega-6 is plentiful to excess in the modern diet, but omega-3 is not and thus should be the object of EFA supplementation. Fortunately, only 1 tablespoon of hempseed oil or 1 ounce of shelled hempseed will supply the needed 2.2 grams of omega-3 (as well as the needed 6.6 grams of omega-6). This is a suitable amount, even for vegetarians, and takes into account a conversion ratio of only 1 percent ALA to DHA, the currently-accepted conversion rate for plant sources of omega-3.

Of course, if you suspect an EFA deficiency, increase your consumption accordingly. However, factors other than minimal intake can decrease the critical ALA to DHA conversion. To recover from an EFA deficiency and maintain good health, it's important to make other changes in your diet as well. A high intake of omega-6 fatty acids, saturated fat, cholesterol, trans-fats, alcohol, and/or a low intake of protein or calories, and/or a deficiency of zinc or copper can reduce the conversion rate. Diabetes and other metabolic disorders also can affect the conversion rate. Those with a lack of certain enzymes, such as ethnic groups with a history of high fish intake, may have difficulty converting ALA to DHA.

Many processed foods have omega-3 in them. Serving sizes vary with the product, from 14 grams for cooking oil to 100 grams for burgers. Both the omega-3 content as well as the suggested serving size will be listed on the label's "nutrition facts." However, if the omega-3 content is not disclosed, the product should be avoided as a reliable source of omega-3s.

Unfortunately, in Canada it is illegal to disclose any omega or EFA content on a product label. Only polyunsaturated, monounsaturated, and saturated fats are permitted to be listed! This is but one of many bizarre anti-consumer laws in Canada that are designed to favor dairy concerns at the expense of public health. Dairy alternatives are actually illegal in Canada, and the land that proudly produces omega-rich canola, flaxseed, and hempseed can't even tell their consumers about it. On the other hand, the U.S. Food and Drug Administration is expected to allow the following health claim on labels: "Consumption of omega-3 fatty acids may reduce the risk of coronary heart disease."

The reduction of EFA intake that occurs naturally in ultra-low-fat and fat-free diets can make people feel hungry and deprived. It also can begin the process of dangerous EFA deficiency. This may cause people on such diets to binge on high-caloric foods to compensate for feeling unsatisfied. The body needs to have some fat in the diet in order to absorb important fat-soluble nutrients such as vitamins A, D, E, and K. Fat-free diets have been correlated with violent, short tempers in human and animal studies. Such diets can cause high cholesterol levels because the body produces excess cholesterol in an attempt to make up for the lack of EFAs. Particularly on a very low-fat diet it is critical to consume enough EFAs to maintain health.

A study of Inuits (Eskimo) found that despite a diet very high in fat they have low rates of cardiovascular disease and diabetes. The reason is the large amount of high-EFA fish that they eat. However, they also have higher levels of contaminants from the fish, highlighting the main problem with getting EFAs from marine sources. Additionally, cooked fish loses much of its original EFAs, some of which convert to toxic trans-fats.

What's a trans-fat? Most everyone is aware that a diet high in saturated fatty acids, such as those found in red meat and dairy products, increases the risk of stroke and heart attack. But fried foods, as well as hydrogenated and refined oils, produce trans-fatty acids, a type of saturated fatty acid that has an effect far worse than normal saturated fats. Trans-fats may also displace the EFAs we should be getting in our diets.

Trans-fatty acids, which are made when a vegetable oil is hydrogenated to make it solid at room temperature, are generally considered the least healthful type of fat to consume. Trans-fats are prevalent in processed foods such as margarine, shortening, chocolate coatings, and baked goods, among many others. They raise blood cholesterol levels and LDL, the "bad" cholesterol, increasing the risk of heart attack.

More importantly, trans-fats interfere with the normal function and use of omega-3 and omega-6. According to the FDA, the average American eats 5 grams of trans-fats every day. That is the equivalent of 1,000 milligrams of omega-3 per day if this amount was replaced with hempseed oil. That is nearly half the amount needed daily by the body.

In fact, trans-fats are so toxic to the body, the FDA is expected to require food labels to disclose trans-fat content in the nutritional facts panel on packaged foods. One FDA scientist believes that removing trans-fats from margarine would save 2,100 deaths annually in the U.S., and removing trans-fats from just 3 percent of cookies and crackers would prevent 5,600 deaths a year. Over twenty years, the health care cost savings alone would be $59 billion.

One way to roughly determine the trans-fat content of a food is to total the number of grams of polyunsaturated, monounsaturated, and saturated fat listed in the "nutrition facts" panel, then subtract it from the "total fat" listed. The remainder is approximately the amount of trans-fat in the product, not counting rounding errors in the "nutrition facts" panel.

Essential fatty acids are not stored or used for energy, as are most fats. In contrast to the shorter-chain and more-saturated fatty acids, they serve not as energy sources but as raw materials for cell structure and as precursors for the synthesis of many of the body's vital biochemicals, including hormones and prostaglandins. Therefore, hempseed oil may be thought of as a "diet" oil, contributing fewer calories than most other oils or fats because it is so rich in EFAs, which are used in cell metabolism instead of being used for energy or stored as fat. Experts say

ESSENTIAL FATTY ACID (EFA) CONTENT OF COMMON OILSEEDS, PER CUP OF WHOLE SEED			
	Total EFAs	Linoleic Acid (omega-6 LA)	Linolenic Acid (omega-3 LNA)
HempNut™	37	28%	9%
Whole hempseed	28	21%	7%
Flax	25	5%	20%
Sesame	22	22%	0
Brazil	16	16%	0
Peanut	14	14%	0
Canola	11	9%	2%
Soybean	10	9%	1%
Hazelnut	10	10%	0
Almond	9	9%	0
Macadamia	7	7%	0
Cashew	3	3%	0
Corn	2	2%	0
Olive	2	2%	0

getting more than 12 to 15 percent of calories from EFAs will actually aid in burning off excess fat and contribute to weight loss.

EFAs also assist in carrying off toxins from the skin, kidneys, lungs, and intestinal tract. They create energy within our cells by transporting oxygen from red blood cells. Converted into hormone-like substances known as prostaglandins, EFAs regulate many cellular functions such as cellular communication, cholesterol production, and blood platelet aggregation. As the different prostaglandins often have opposite effects, they are needed by the body in a delicate balance obtained from a balanced intake of the two essential fatty acids, omega-6 and omega-3. For instance, the prostaglandins that wind up the body's response to stress are all made by omega-6 fatty acids, and the ones that wind down the body's response to stress are nearly all made by omega-3 fatty acids. Not surprisingly, stress-related diseases tend to respond to omega-3 supplementation.

Omega-3 content comparison of various foods, per uncooked 1-oz. portion (28g)

	milligrams of omega-3 in a 1-oz. portion
HempNut™	2,500
Chinook salmon	556
Atlantic farmed salmon	556
Atlantic wild salmon	435
Pink salmon	400
Farmed trout	357
Wild trout	313
White tuna, canned	270
Sockeye salmon	250
Mackerel	208
Flounder/sole	156
Fresh tuna	149
Alaskan king crab	130
Shrimp	100
Light tuna, canned	96
Atlantic cod	88
Wild catfish	74
Farmed catfish	56
Lobster	44

In the body, some omega-6 and omega-3 is changed into other forms of polyunsaturated fatty acids, including two which are rare: gamma-linolenic acid ("GLA," an omega-6 fatty acid, C18:3w6) and stearidonic acid ("SDA," an omega-3 fatty acid, 18:4w3), respectively. This process happens by the enzymatic action of delta-6-desaturase.

GLA is found in minute quantities in most animal fats. Oats, barley, and wheat germ also contain small amounts, as does human milk. Good sources of GLA include hempseed and hempseed oil (2 to 6 percent in hempseed oil), blue-green algae (spirulina), evening primrose oil, black currant seed oil, borage oil, and some fungal oils. The alleviating action of GLA on psoriasis, atopic eczema, and mastalgia already is well documented; GLA preparations are frequently prescribed for the treatment of the latter two disorders. GLA also has been researched for its beneficial effects in cardiovascular, psychiatric, and immunological disorders. Stearidonic acid (SDA) makes up as much as 2 to 4 percent of some hempseed oils and is important in the human diet. Trans-fatty acids inhibit the production of GLA and SDA, which serve as intermediaries in the formation of longer-chain fatty acids and vital hormone-like prostaglandins in the body.

Omega-3 is the building block of the longer-chain fatty acids EPA (eicosapentaenoic acid) and DHA (docosahexaenoic acid), found naturally in cold-water fatty fish such as salmon, tuna, mackerel, sardines, and herring. The analogous product derived from omega-6 is the longer-chain fatty acid AA (arachidonic acid), which has effects opposite those of DHA. Foods high in AA include meat and shellfish, and they may be a contributing factor to menstrual cramps.

Vegetarians and others who do not eat fish can easily obtain omega-3 and omega-6 fatty acids through shelled hempseed or hempseed oil. Fish oil and flaxseed oil are high in omega-3 but low in omega-6. Fish oil may also be high in cholesterol and ocean pollutants, and it is increasingly farmed, which can provide less EFAs than the wild fish traditionally used for food. (To be fair, flaxseed is high in lignins, a phytoestrogen good for preventing cancer, osteoporosis, and menstrual and menopause complications. It also has antibacterial and antiviral properties. Fish has a higher rate of conversion than flaxseed or hempseed to the actual omega-3 products the body uses; that is, the conversion rate of ALA to DHA for flaxseed is about 1 percent. Ironically, the high omega-3 content in fish is from the plankton it eats, not the fish itself.)

A deficiency of omega-6 fatty acids can result in disorders such as arthritis, behavior disturbances, cardiovascular problems, excessive thirst, hair loss, infection, kidney and liver degeneration, miscarriage, poor circulation and glandular function, premenstrual syndrome, reduced sperm motility and impotence in men, slow growth and wound healing, and skin diseases. However, for twenty years scientists have warned that overconsumption of omega-6 relative to omega-3 can actually have ill effects, so they must be balanced. The excess arachidonic acid (AA) from omega-6 creates inflammation and, more importantly, increased blood clotting, which can cause a heart attack, stroke, or embolism. In the last forty years the American diet has become loaded with excess omega-6 from corn and soybean oil, margarine, and similar processed fats. At the same time, Americans eat 500 milligrams of omega-3 per day less than they need, for an omega-

6:omega-3 ratio of 50:1, instead of the recommended 3:1 ratio. The Standard American Diet (SAD) is just that: sad. And with cardiovascular disease the number one killer in the U.S., accounting for 40 percent of deaths, it may literally be killing us!

Lack of omega-3 fatty acids have been implicated in such problems as:

Alzheimer's	emphysema
arrhythmia	hypertension
asthma	immune weakness
atherosclerosis	inflammation
attention deficit/	lack of coordination
hyperactivity disorder	learning disabilities
bipolar disorder	memory loss
breast cancer	migraine headaches
colon cancer	myocardial infarction
coronary heart disease	abnormal brain and eye develop-
Crohn's disease	ment in infants and children
cystic fibrosis	obesity
dementia	prostate cancer
depression	psoriasis
diabetes	rheumatoid arthritis
dry skin	schizophrenia
elevated serum triglycerides	sudden cardiac death

Therefore, increasing EFA consumption can likely help treat and possibly prevent these conditions. Two studies found that the omega-3 product EPA (eicosapentaenoic acid) was very powerful in helping reduce depression in patients who previously didn't respond to antidepressants.

Besides protein and EFAs, other important nutrients found in shelled hempseed are lecithin, choline, inositol, and phytosterols:

- Lecithin is a type of lipid found in the protective sheaths surrounding the brain and nervous system. It also aids in the breakdown of fats and enhances liver activity and enzyme production.

- Produced from lecithin, choline is needed for nerve impulses from the brain throughout the nervous system and for liver and gall bladder function. Its derivative acetylcholine, lacking in Alzheimer's patients, is crucial for short-term memory.

- Inositol promotes hair growth, reduces cholesterol levels, prevents artery hardening, and is calming to the nervous system.
- Phytosterols, sometimes described as "plant hormones" or phytoestrogens, affect cholesterol absorption, hormone regulation, and cell metabolism.

Shelled hempseed also is high in minerals such as potassium, calcium, magnesium, sulfur, iron, and zinc:

- Potassium supports the nervous system and regular heart rhythm and, with the help of sodium, aids in the body's balance of water.
- Calcium also is essential for a regular heartbeat, strong teeth and bones, and nerve impulses.
- Magnesium is needed to transmit the nerve and muscle messages.
- Sulfur helps the body resist bacterial invasion and protects it against toxic substances.
- Moderate amounts of iron facilitate the production of red blood cells and energy.
- Zinc is important for a healthy reproductive system and the male prostate gland. It improves wound healing and strengthens the immune system.

Of special interest to diabetics, the glycemic index of shelled hempseed is considered low, as it is very low in carbohydrates and full of nutrients that moderate blood sugar.

Does any other food provide such a significant range of health-promoting nutrients? Undoubtedly hempseed oil and shelled hempseed would be helpful in preventing many illnesses and diseases common in the Western world today. And with great taste, of course!

Hempseed oil is one of the best vegetarian sources of essential fatty acids.
Photo: Larry Stanley

Chapter 6

Hempseed: Mankind's Original Nutraceutical

Throughout history hempseed has been recognized for its medicinal properties still worthy of consideration today. As an anti-inflammatory, it soothes and reduces inflammation. As an antiseptic, it prevents bacterial growth, inhibits pathogens, and counters sepsis. As a demulcent, it soothes irritated tissues, especially of the mucus membranes. As a diuretic, it increases urine by promoting activity of the kidneys and bladder. As an emollient, it's used externally to soothe, soften, and protect the skin. Because it is a hypotensive, it lowers high blood pressure. As a laxative, it stimulates bowel action; particularly whole hempseed due to its fiber and soothing qualities. And as a tonic, it promotes general health and well-being, supports all organs, and builds energy and strength.

The oldest references to hempseed as an herbal medicine date back to the Chinese pharmacopoeia more than two thousand years ago. During the first century A.D., the famous Chinese surgeon Hua T'o made an effective anesthetic from hempseed and wine, which was used during difficult abdominal surgeries. In first-century Rome, Emperor Nero's physician, Dioscorides, recommended hempseed juice (oil) as a remedy for earaches. Another physician, Pliny the Elder, suggested hempseed juice to expel insects and worms from the ear and relieve constipation in farm animals. The seed also was prescribed to remedy gout.

During the Ming dynasty (1368–1644), a text called *Ri Yong Ben Cao (Household Materia Medica)* included hempseed as medicine, and a large section of the *Pen T'sao Kang Mu* pharmacopoeia was devoted to hempseed. It was classified as a "superior" medicine, inherently nontoxic and suitable for long-term use.

The *Pen T'sao* states that hempseed will "aid in the growth of the body's muscle fiber . . . [and] increase the flow of mother's milk," and that "it can be used to hasten childbirth, where the delivery is troubled with complications or is overdue." Quoting books even older, it proclaims that whole hempseed is useful "to mend and help all of the central areas and benefit the chi [life force]." The book also includes a "Formula to Build Up an Age-Enduring Supply of Beneficial Qi" (*Nai*

Lao Yi Qi) where two liters of hempseed and one liter of soybeans are boiled together, then slowly fried until they become a dried powder, which is rolled up with honey to form pills taken twice daily.

In the 1794 edition of the *Edinburgh New Dispensatory*, British herbalist Nicholas Culpeper referred to an emulsion of hempseed oil in milk that was given as treatment for venereal disease and as a cough remedy. He also wrote, "[An] emulsion or decoction of the seed ... eases colic and allays the troublesome humours in the bowels and stays [stops] bleeding at the mouth, nose and other places."

Around the turn of the nineteenth century, hempseed was widely consumed in China as a longevity tonic to prevent old age and "firm the flesh." Boils were treated with a poultice of ground hempseed and honey. A variety of *ma zi* (hemp plant) that produced larger, pea-sized hempseed was considered of the highest quality and is being re-established today in a special years-long natural breeding program to develop a very large hempseed especially for food, funded by the author.

In traditional Chinese medicine, hempseed is classified as being sweet and neutral, affecting the stomach, spleen, and large intestines. It is indicated for dysentery and has been used as a diuretic agent and to kill worms. The EFAs in hempseed lubricate and nourish the colon. Hempseed is still included in patent formulas for its laxative properties, a remedy gentle enough for the elderly and postpartum women.

Hempseed also is prescribed to aid menstrual irregularities, childbirth, prolapsed uterus, postpartum recovery, fever reduction, severe vomiting, "blood deficiency," constipation due to intestinal dryness, and wound healing. Hempseed oil has been used topically for sores, burns, sulfur poisoning, hair loss, dry throat, and ulcerations.

Traditional Chinese formulas including hempseed are *Ma-zi-ren-wan* (cannabis seed pills) for constipation with hemorrhoids, and *Wan-bing-hui-chun* (intestine moistening decoction) for the treatment of constipation. They are available in Asian medicine shops. The average intake of hempseed in a patent medicine is nine to fifteen grams.

Conditions Helped by Hempseed Oil's Essential Fatty Acids (EFAs)

Since the late 1970s, dozens of studies have shown the power of omega-3 and/or omega-6 fatty acids in preventing or treating many illnesses and conditions. These studies have been published in such respected medical journals as *The*

Lancet, Annals of Internal Medicine, Journal of the American Medical Association, American Journal of Cardiology, New England Journal of Medicine, British Medical Journal, American Journal of Epidemiology, Archives of Internal Medicine, Archives of General Psychiatry, Nutrition Today, Medical Journal of Australia, Cancer, Journal of Lipid Research, Lipids, American Journal of Clinical Nutrition, American Journal of Health-System Pharmacy, Nutrition Reviews, and *British Journal of Nutrition*. In these studies omega-3 was found useful for treating conditions as varied as:

abnormal brain and eye development in infants and children

acne

aggression

allergies

Alzheimer's disease

arterial inelasticity

asthma

atherosclerosis

atopic dermatitis

attention deficit/hyperactivity disorder

bipolar disorder

birth complications

blood viscosity

breast cancer

cardiac arrhythmia

cardiac stenosis

cerebral palsy

colon cancer

coronary heart disease

Crohn's disease

cyclic breast pain

cystic fibrosis

dementia

depression

diabetes mellitus

dry skin

dyslexia

eczema

elevated serum triglycerides

emphysema

erythema

excessive thirst

fibrocystic breasts

fingernail and hair problems

gastric ulcers

growth retardation (fetal/infant/child)

hair discoloration, thinning and loss

hypercholesterolemia (high cholesterol)

hypertension (high blood pressure)

immune weakness

impotence

increased transepidermal water loss

infection

inflammation and auto-immune diseases

kidney and liver degeneration

lack of coordination

learning disabilities

low birth weight

lupus erythmatosis

memory loss

menopause complications

menstrual bleeding, abnormal

menstrual cramps

migraine headaches

miscarriage

multiple sclerosis

myocardial infarction (heart attack)

obesity

osteoporosis

platelet stickiness or aggregation

poor circulation and glandular function

pre-eclampsia

premature birth

premenstrual syndrome

prostaglandin and hormone production

prostate cancer

psoriasis

reduced sperm motility

rheumatoid arthritis

scaly epidermis

schizophrenia

sebaceous duct hyperkeratosis

sebaceous gland hypertrophy

side effects of chemotherapy

slow growth

slow wound healing

stroke

sudden cardiac death

vasoconstriction

weakened cutaneous capillaries

One study found that it was also important to consume vitamin E with omega-3s in order to prevent oxidation (rancidity). Although most of the studies used omega-3 from fish or flaxseed oils, hempseed oil is likely acceptable as well, since it is 20 percent omega-3.

The following conditions may be helped by adding EFAs in the form of hempseed oil or shelled hempseed to the diet. This is for informational purposes only and is not a diagnosis or recommendation, which of course should only be prescribed under the advice of a physician.

Addiction: Nobel-prize nominee Dr. Johanna Budwig suggests that EFAs have been helpful in treating addictions to alcohol, cigarettes, drugs, and sex-and-violence patterns. EFAs enable a person to manage stress better: nerve and brain functions stabilize, and the electric currents across the brain's cell membranes increase, inducing a person to feel calmer and more focused.

Arthritis and other inflammatory disorders: GLA reduces inflammation in joints and "morning stiffness," while omega-3 has demonstrated anti-inflammatory effects in conditions such as "tennis elbow," bladder infection, ulcerative colitis, and Crohn's disease, a chronic inflammation of the bowel. It's now known that EFAs can be used to treat acute joint inflammation without nonsteroidal anti-inflammatory drugs, the typical regime.

Attention deficit, hyperactivity, and other mental disorders: EFAs are critical for the healthy functioning of the brain cell membranes, as most of the brain's cell walls are composed of fats. Adequate amounts of EFAs maintain the brain cells' fluid and flexible condition. Children require both omega-6 and omega-3 for proper brain maturation. A deficiency in omega-3, in particular, can contribute to learning disabilities. Research using supplementation of omega-3 and omega-6 indicates that they are useful in the treatment of attention deficit disorder, depression, and schizophrenia. In countries where the people eat much omega-3 there is 90 percent less clinical depression.

Cancer: Improving cellular utilization of oxygen, omega-3 reduces tumor formation and slows tumor growth by decreasing the metastasis of cancer cells. Cancer cells and tissue have lower GLA and omega-6 levels than healthy tissue, and blood samples taken from cancer patients were lacking in EFAs. When a diet high in EFAs and skim milk protein was fed to the cancer patients, tumors receded, and many patients recovered during a three-month period. Saturated fats and refined vegetable oils are believed to be contributing factors in cancer, as are trans-fatty acids.

Cardiovascular diseases: Most cardiovascular diseases are caused by the formation of arterial plaque, the deposit of hardened material on the interior walls of arteries. This process may eventually block blood flow and cause arteriosclerosis and strokes. LDL cholesterol, a sticky substance present in the blood, has been identified as one of the main contributors to it. Dietary treatment with daily doses of omega-6 and GLA, which correspond roughly to four teaspoons of hempseed oil, has resulted in a decrease of elevated blood levels of both LDL and total cholesterol. Omega-3 is useful for maintaining flexible blood vessels, membranes, and cells. People who eat nuts at least one to four times per week have a 22 percent lower risk of heart attack and heart disease compared to those who eat nuts less than once a week.

Constipation: Traditional Chinese medicine maintains that large quantities of whole hempseed act as a demulcent laxative, soothing and lubricating the bowels, and thus is useful in the prevention of constipation. Since whole hempseed is 40 percent shell, fiber is likely the active ingredient.

Diabetes: Elevated blood sugar levels, a condition of diabetes, can cause an EFA deficiency in the body. With age-onset diabetes, symptoms of numbness and tingling in the extremities can be alleviated with a daily intake of 360 milligrams GLA, the equivalent of three teaspoons of hempseed oil or six teaspoons of shelled hempseed.

Diarrhea: Hempseed tea soothes irritated intestines and provides nutrients during bouts of diarrhea. Eaten in moderate amounts as gruel, it can help solidify the stool. EFAs have been shown to reduce infant colitis in premature babies.

Earache: Hempseed oil has been used in eardrops to loosen earwax, reduce pain, and fight infection.

Edema: EFAs assist the kidneys in eliminating excess tissue water. Hempseed is also a diuretic, relieving the swelling of edema.

Fatigue: EFAs help maintain alertness. EFA deficiency can contribute to anemia, which is accompanied by loss of energy. EFAs shorten the time tired muscles need for recovery by assisting the conversion of lactic acid to carbon dioxide and water. Athletes ingesting EFAs report an increase of stamina and strength, higher performance levels, and quicker recovery of muscle fatigue, sprains, and bruises.

Immune deficiency: In order to resist and recover from infection, the body needs globular-shaped protein to produce antibodies. Hempseed is rich in the globular proteins albumin and edestin, as well as EFAs, all of which assist immune response. EFAs improve the metabolic rate, thus helping to prevent the buildup of harmful yeasts and bacteria. They also strengthen cellular membranes, making them less susceptible to infection.

Infant and child health: Hempseed is a galactagogue and helps to increase production of a nursing mother's milk. Infant formulas are required to be fortified with EFAs, which are essential for the development of the pre- and post-natal baby. When omega-3 and omega-6 are deficient in an infant's or child's diet, growth is slowed, especially growth of the nervous system, brain, and eyes. In addition, skin problems may occur, learning is slowed, and colic and diarrhea are more common. Pregnant and nursing mothers should include fresh hempseed oil in their diets, as the fetus and nursing baby drain the mother's body of EFAs. One study found that the babies of mothers who ate more EFAs had a lower incidence of cerebral palsy. Another study found that it took only six hours after the consumption of EFAs for them to appear in breast milk, and they remained for ten to twenty-four hours, and in some cases up to three days. The mothers' high omega-3 levels decreased the incidence of infants born prematurely; increased average birth weight by eight ounces; increased placenta weight, birth length, and head circumference; and improved the intelligence of eighteen-month-old babies. The diet of the culture with the highest average birth weights in the world is fish based. Clearly, a mother's consumption of EFAs during and after pregnancy gives the new baby a head start on life.

Menopause: Dry skin, vaginal dryness, night sweats, hormone production, hot flashes, and moodiness are improved with EFAs.

Multiple Sclerosis: EFAs slow nerve deterioration. Studies show that supplementation of EFAs can improve MS. In geographical areas where EFA consumption is adequate, MS is rare.

Neurodermitis and skin ailments: There is a clear connection between healthy skin and EFA intake. Patients with neurodermitis show a deficiency of omega-6 and omega-3 fatty acids. It's assumed that the enzymatic synthesis of GLA and SDA, and subsequently of prostaglandins, is inhibited. A deficiency in omega-6 is also associated with eczema and psoriasis in humans and dogs, as omega-6 helps regulate water loss through the skin. Due to its high content of omega-6 and GLA, hempseed oil can assist in the treatment of these disorders. The daily oral intake found to improve the skin condition over a twelve-week period corresponds to about four teaspoons of hempseed oil or one and one-half ounces of shelled hempseed. Another study showed improvement through the external application of an ointment containing GLA, so a hempseed oil salve might be useful. Yet another found that GLA can reduce the redness, swelling, and pain caused by sunburn. Hempseed oil taken internally and applied topically can relieve itching of the skin, speed its healing process, and prevent dry, cracked skin as well as stretch marks. Rejuvenative, it not only keeps the skin smooth and velvety but can actually slow the skin's aging process. Due to its easy and high absorption into the skin, hempseed oil is a perfect carrier for topical medicines; for the same reason, however, it is not a good carrier for sunblock.

Obesity: Using "good" fats high in EFAs can help reduce hunger. Fat in the small intestine stimulates the release of chemical transmitters that make the brain feel satisfied and thus the stomach less hungry. EFAs help break down excess saturated fat by increasing the metabolic rate.

Osteoporosis: Bone loss is a serious concern for the elderly and often is associated with kidney and artery calcification. EFA supplementation improves calcium absorption and enhances overall bone strength.

Premenstrual syndrome: PMS can manifest in painful muscular tension, swelling of the breasts, nervousness, irritability, and depression. Research indicates that women with PMS suffer from a metabolic weakness converting omega-6 into GLA, and subsequently into prostaglandins. An intake of 1.37 grams omega-6 and 156 milligrams GLA over a period of twelve weeks has been shown to significantly improve PMS symptoms. This intake corresponds to one teaspoon of hempseed oil or two teaspoons of shelled hempseed per day.

Tuberculosis: Thirty years of experience in Czechoslovakia found that a diet appropriate for tuberculosis must be high in protein. The study states that "[g]round hempseeds extracted by milk at a temperature from 60 to 89°C prove to be—even in their smallest doses—an utmost effective remedy," and that hempseed is the "only food that can successfully treat the consumptive disease tuberculosis." EFAs help restore wasting bodies by improving the damaged immune systems. They also make it easier for the patient to liquefy and expel mucus that has built up in the lungs.

Even pets can benefit from hempseed oil. It has long been known that birds thrive and seek out hempseed, either in birdfeed or in the wild. For centuries many bird hunters have known that their best bet was to lie in wait near a stand of wild hemp. The Birdman of Alcatraz wrote "Hempseed makes the song birds sing." I have personally seen wild and domesticated birds suddenly become very quick to devour and hoard shelled hempseed when offered to them, more so than with any other feed.

Animals deficient in EFAs have slower wound healing, dry, scaly skin, and a dull, brittle coat. Hempseed oil added to the diet or directly to the hair of the affected area has a remarkable effect on many conditions, yet another reason to add hempseed oil to your pet's diet or hempseed to your bird's feed. Cats should not be fed high-omega-6 oils such as corn, soy, canola, hempseed, or flaxseed, since due to their history as pure carnivores they lack the enzyme for metabolizing plant-based omega-6 and may develop toxicity from it.

Introduced in 1994, Hempeh Burger® was the first hemp burger.

The first hemp-based dairy alternative, originally called HempRella®.

The first hempseed food to make the permissible health claim "Helps support healthy heart, brain, lung, and immune function."

Photos this page: Larry Stanley

Chapter 7

Nature's Perfect Oil

The domestic, medicinal, and industrial use of hempseed oil (or "hemp oil") has been long, extensive, and widespread. Even the short film *Hemp for Victory*, made in 1942 by the U.S. Department of Agriculture, begins: "Since before ancient times, hemp has been in service to mankind."

Considered the brightest lamp oil, hempseed oil lit the lamps of the legendary Aladdin as well as Abraham the Prophet. Burning cleanly, it produces no smoke and does not hurt the eyes. The first diesel engines ran on hempseed oil, an industrial product with many uses common in Europe for centuries.

Because hemp has long been the dominant fiber used to make canvas, sails, clothes, rope, and paper, the seed from those hemp fiber plants was plentiful and useful, yielding as much as 1.5 tons per acre. For instance, the paint and varnish industry used hempseed oil as a drying agent. From 1935 to 1937, ninety thousand tons of hempseed were imported into the U.S. to make oil for this purpose alone.

But nutrition is where hempseed oil really shines! Consider for a moment how good hemp fiber is for paper, clothes, and rope. Think of the thousands of houses built with hemp particle board, concrete, and stucco, and remember how important hempseed oil has been throughout history. Now realize this: the future for industrial hemp, the biggest potential for its economic value and human utility, is in none of these!

I believe the main reason hemp will be grown anew is for its unique nutraceuticals, especially the plentiful essential fatty acids omega-3, gamma-linoleic acid (GLA), and stearidonic acid (SDA). Well, that and the beautifully fragrant terpenes captured from water distillation of the flowers. It has a delicious, clary sage-like scent, with seemingly universal appeal. This cannabis essential oil is used today in perfumes and as a flavoring for foods and beverages throughout Europe.

Hempseed oil is unusually high in polyunsaturated fatty acids (70 to 80 percent), while its low content of saturated fatty acids (less than 10 percent) compares favorably with even the least saturated vegetable oils. Hempseed oil contains approximately 60 percent omega-6 and 20 percent omega-3 essential fatty acids, in a ratio of 3:1, the same ratio they are found in the body.

It takes about five pounds of whole hempseed to make one pound of hempseed oil. The byproduct is "presscake," or more accurately, "de-fatted hempseed meal," sometimes marketed as "hemp flour" or "hemp protein." This byproduct is lower in EFAs than whole hempseed but higher in protein and fiber.

Its high degree of unsaturation renders hempseed oil sensitive to air, heat, and light. Unsaturated molecules attract oxygen; the ensuing oxidation causes rancidity accelerated by exposure to high temperatures or light.

Hempseed oil is suitable for cooking at temperatures up to 475°F for no longer than thirty minutes. This ability to withstand heat is quite unique among polyunsaturated fats, since most—like canola, soy, flax, and fish oils—convert to transfats when heated at much lower temperatures for far less time. Even fish, when cooked, can convert its omega-3 to trans-fats. With its unique heat resistance of the fatty acid and a unique, efficient protein molecule, hempseed truly is ideal for service to mankind. Hemp is a one-of-a-kind plant!

Combining hempseed oil with a high-temperature-stable cooking oil increases the ability of the hempseed oil to withstand heat and provides the most "good" fat and fewest trans-fats from cooking. An ideal oil for this is avocado oil, with its smoke point 50 percent higher than olive oil and a large percentage of monounsaturated fatty acids, which have a positive effect on health. Hempseed oil may be added at a 5 to 10 percent level in the avocado oil to obtain a good amount of omega-3 (140 to 280 mg per 14-gram serving) but still withstand the heat of normal cooking. That's three to six tablespoons of hempseed oil per quart of avocado oil.

The use of this avocado/hempseed oil blend is perhaps the most healthful choice possible, since it will displace the use of other less-healthful cooking oils, such as the saturated fat and cholesterol found in butter, trans-fats found in margarine and shortening, and the far less-stable polyunsaturated oils, such as canola and soy, which are loaded with an excess of omega-6 and convert to trans-fats when heated.

Unrefined hempseed oil, green in color due to chlorophyll, is delicious as a table oil, in salad dressings, for dipping bread, or in any recipe calling for oil. Better food stores sell hempseed oil in bottles and gel capsules.

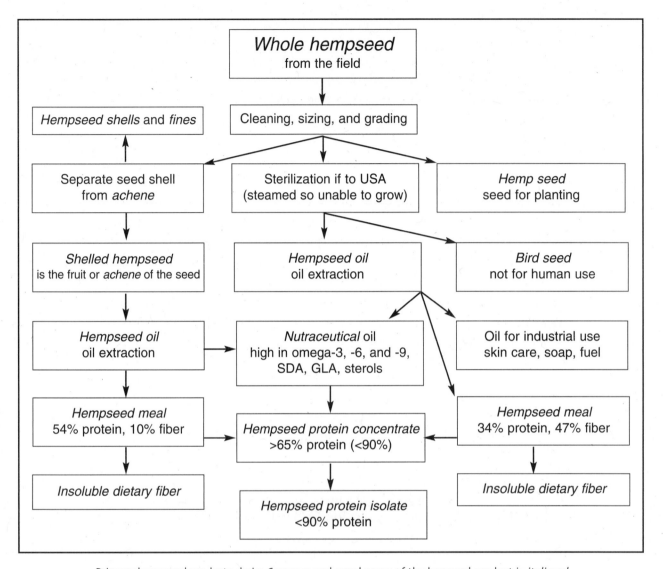

Primary hempseed products chain. Common and usual name of the hemseed product is *italiczed*.

Hempseed oil is made like other common vegetable oils. Typically, whole hempseed is put in a special press that literally squeezes the oil from it. Best extracted mechanically in a light- and oxygen-free environment, hempseed oil should be stabilized with antioxidants such as vitamin E (tocopherol), vitamin A (carotene), or rosemary extract to prevent rancidity. The package should be topped off with an inert gas, such as nitrogen or argon, and kept from heat and light. Maximum ripening of the hempseed and removal of immature seeds are important for the production of quality oil. Large, dark, plump-looking seeds make the best oil.

Unrefined hempseed oil extracted by the cold-pressing methods described above varies in color from off-yellow to dark green and has a pleasant, nutty taste, sometimes accompanied by a touch of bitterness. Oil that tastes "off," with a "fishy" or a "paint" smell, is rancid and should be discarded.

As the manufacturing quality will greatly impact the quality of the oil, it is advisable to purchase only the highest-quality hempseed oil. Whereas hempseed oil is expensive in comparison to refined, solvent-extracted, or heat-pressed oils, it is superior in nutritional value. It is estimated that if cultivated again in the U.S., its cost will be comparable to that of corn oil.

Hempseed oil is best stored in the freezer (it will stay fluid and does not need to be defrosted before using). Anywhere from one teaspoon to three tablespoons is the suggested daily intake for adults. Children can use half that amount. A breast-fed baby will obtain the benefits of hempseed oil through the mother's milk.

Besides being an incredibly nutrient-dense food, wonderful and effective skin care products are made with hempseed oil. Non-greasy, since it is quickly absorbed and blessed with superior "slippery" qualities, it is used in lip balm, lipstick, lotion, massage oil, shampoo, conditioner, hair treatment, and as a carrier for topical medicines.

The easy skin absorption of hempseed oil makes it a good carrier for other healthy ingredients.

That old favorite, peanut butter, is made more nutritious by adding shelled hempseed.

A chocolate energy bar with shelled hempseed, as delicious as it is nutritious.

Photos this page: Larry Stanley

Another early drawing of various aspects of Cannabis sativa L.

Chapter 8

From Ancient Hempseed to Modern "HempNut"

Botanically speaking, hempseed is a tiny, egg-shaped fruit, or achene, forming in the tops of female cannabis flowers. It's protected by a thin, hard shell with a brown and black or gray marbled pattern. The size of whole hempseed can vary from 2 to 60 grams per one thousand seeds. Each seed contains a whitish embryo, which is the actual shelled hempseed. It's about the size of a sesame seed, or a little larger.

To be imported into the United States, the Department of Agriculture requires that whole hempseed be sterilized so it won't grow. Shelling of the hempseed satisfies the requirement as well. Consisting mainly of fiber, and some chlorophyll with mature seeds, the edible shell acts as roughage. It can stick between your teeth and taste gritty.

Hempseed is free of psychoactive properties. When it is harvested, however, minute amounts of THC in the flowers' resin, called adherent, may cling to the outside of the hempseed shell, so low as to be in the parts-per-million and -billion range. The adherent can be easily removed by cleaning or shelling the seed.

Shelled from hempseed grown by low-THC plants, shelled hempseed typically has no detectable THC residue and therefore is exempt from drug laws. Because it does not germinate or grow, shelled hempseed can be imported into the United States without heat sterilization, which helps protect more of the seed's nutritional value and quality.

EFA proponent Dr. Udo Erasmus states that "hemp butter puts our peanut butter to shame for nutritional value." A mere handful of shelled hempseed daily provides the minimum requirement of protein for adults.

Hempseed is full of enzymes, and in fact enzymes were first discovered in hempseed. Heat and air naturally diminish enzyme strength, but fresh hempseed often can have a sharp taste, which is due to enzymes. Old hempseed kernels can have an orange color, the result of the enzyme lipase digesting fat in the seed. Besides lipase, the enzyme protease is found in hempseed, among others.

Hempseed varies greatly in size, from 2 to 60 grams per 1,000 seeds. The largest seeds pictured here are the first specifically bred for use in hempseed foods, in a breeding project funded by the author.
Photo: Robert C. Clarke— International Hemp Association

Even chocolate chip cookies can be made tastier by adding shelled hempseed.

Energy bars are the most popular hempseed food, with at least 15 companies producing them worldwide.

Chapter 9

Cooking with Shelled Hempseed

Recipes by Brigitte Mars, edited by Christina Pirello

Cooking with hempseed? As in recipes? Aren't they simply lovely little seeds to be sprinkled on various dishes—you know, lightly toasted or made into tasty condiments? Yes, and that can be splendid. You'll even find some of those delicious recipes in this book. But hempseed is so much more than that, and, as outlined in the first eight chapters of this book, can provide more nutrition than just about any other plant food—and most animal foods, too!

I was introduced to hempseed years ago, but I never really paid much attention to it. Sure, I occasionally sprinkled the seeds on my food and thought they had a wonderful, nutty flavor, but I didn't cook with them. Then Richard asked me to edit the recipes for this book and maybe add a few of my own. Now it was time for me to see what he'd been talking about these many years—if hempseed and oil were, in fact, all he said.

I've been cooking with and teaching about whole natural foods for more than twenty years and have been enchanted by a lot of products over that time. But cooking with hempseed and oil was love at first bite. Sensually rich and buttery, hempseed and oil added a depth of flavor to just about every recipe I prepared. I was hooked.

There was one challenge. How could I take this ancient food, unfamiliar to many modern people, and show how smoothly and easily it could be incorporated into our daily diet and how deliciously it could nourish us? The answer came easily enough: the way I've always introduced people to natural cooking—in friendly, familiar, irresistible recipes.

As I've edited and added to the dishes in this book, I've surprised myself on more than one occasion with the results. Each time, I'd pick up the phone and call Richard, bubbling with excitement, asking the same question: Did he know that hempseed and oil could do all of these things? His amused, knowing chuckle was always my answer. After many sessions in the kitchen, testing and experimenting,

I've come to see what he was so excited about years ago when he first told me that hempseed is the food of the future. I may have laughed then, but as usual in our long friendship, he's having the last laugh. And we're all the better for it.

Wait until you try some of these recipes. From breakfast ideas and beverages to soups, salads, entrées, and yes, desserts, hempseed is not only delicious and incredibly nutrient-dense, it's surprisingly versatile. I can think of very few recipes where it wouldn't add something marvelous. How cool is that? These beauties are destined for much more than a sprinkle a day!

Christina Pirello,
editor

HempNut Recipes

by Brigitte Mars

beverages

You may not think of hempseed when you think of beverages, but perhaps you should. By incorporating it into creamy shakes, smoothies, and various other beverages, we add extraordinary nutrients like omega-3 and protein to our diet. It gets even better: liquids have the uncanny ability to carry nutrients deep into the body, nourishing us on many levels. They are a great vehicle for essential vitamins and minerals; they digest easily; and we assimilate them more efficiently. And did I mention that these beverage recipes are incredibly delicious?

—Christina

breakfast

Your mother was right, at least about this: breakfast is the most important meal of the day. After a night of rest, our bodies need some nutrients to face the challenges of daily life. How we nourish ourselves in the morning can determine our emotional and physical well-being for the day. Hard-to-digest foods, dense, heavy protein, dry toast, butter, and simple sugars will make us feel tired and lethargic and put us on the roller coaster of emotional ups and downs that will leave us exhausted and depleted by lunchtime.

What constitutes a healthy breakfast? Not bacon and eggs or drive-through sandwiches, that's for sure. Soft, easy-to-digest, high-protein foods that are rich in omega-3s are the best choices for getting us off to a good start each day. These kinds of foods help us to feel gently nourished, deeply satisfied, and calmly grounded.

—Christina

Mango Shake

Makes 3 to 4 servings.

2 ripe bananas, cut into chunks

1 large ripe mango, peeled and cut into chunks

1 cup apple juice

1 cup herb tea of your choice (something with lemon essence
      is especially nice)

½ cup vanilla soymilk

¼ cup shelled hempseed

¼ cup brown rice syrup or pure maple syrup

½ teaspoon pure vanilla extract

¼ teaspoon ground cardamom

¼ teaspoon ground cinnamon

½ to 1 cup chopped ice

Place all the ingredients except the ice in a blender and purée until smooth. Slowly add the ice to achieve the desired thickness. More ice will create a thicker, "smoothie" consistency; less will result in a thinner, milkshake-like consistency. Serve immediately or chilled.

Variations:

• By using the freshest fruits available, you can create as many delicious shakes as the seasons permit. Fresh berries, peaches, apricots, and plums are just some of the many options to use in addition to or instead of the banana and/or mango.

• Freeze the fruit before blending for an icy smoothie treat.

Here is a refreshing, creamy, and delicately sweet smoothie. It's packed with vitamins and minerals and contains complete protein and essential fatty acids from the hempseed. It's a powerful way to start the day, or simply enjoy it anytime as a nutritious snack.

HempNut Milk

Makes 1 quart

1 cup shelled hempseed
1 to 3 tablespoons brown rice syrup
1 teaspoon pure vanilla extract
Juice of ½ fresh lemon (about 1½ tablespoons)
Pinch of sea salt
1 quart spring or filtered water

Process all the ingredients except the water in a blender. Add the water gradually, blending for 3 minutes. Strain. Use HempNut Milk to replace dairy or other milks in recipes. It will keep, refrigerated, for about one week.

Variation: Adjust the sweetness of the milk by increasing or decreasing the amount of rice syrup used.

Need a substitute for milk? Try this version of seed milk. Lightly sweet and more delicate than nut milks, hempseed milk packs an unparalleled nutritional punch.

Spiced Coffee Drink

4 cups spring water
4 teaspoons instant grain coffee
1 teaspoon toasted shelled hempseed (see note below)
½ teaspoon ground cinnamon
½ teaspoon powdered ginger
½ teaspoon broken cardamom pods
½ teaspoon star anise

Bring the water to a boil in a saucepan and whisk in the grain coffee and hempseed. Crush the other ingredients with a mortar and pestle or pulse them in a spice grinder to create a coarse powder. Crush the spices just enough to release their aroma and stir into the simmering grain coffee. Remove from the heat and steep 10 minutes. Strain to refine the texture of the coffee. Serve with brown rice syrup and vanilla soymilk on the side, if desired.

Note: To pan toast hempseed, simply place a dry skillet over medium heat. When the skillet is hot, add the hempseed. Cook and stir until fragrant, about 2 minutes.

Want the earthy taste of coffee but not the nerve-shattering kick of caffeine? Try this delicious coffee substitute. It's just spicy enough to grab your attention but won't set your teeth on edge.

Lassi

1 cup plain soy yogurt
1 ripe banana, cut into chunks
¼ cup shelled hempseed
1 tablespoon rose water (see note below)
2 teaspoons brown rice syrup or pure maple syrup
Pinch of ground cardamom

Place all the ingredients in a blender and purée until smooth. Serve at room temperature or lightly chilled.

Note: Rose water can be found in specialty shops and Middle Eastern markets.

Creamy and rich, lightly scented with rose water, this fragrant treat is as good for you as it is delicious. It's a power-packed way to start any active day.

Omega Smoothie

Makes 1 to 2 smoothies

2 cups frozen raspberries or strawberries
1 cup vanilla soymilk
2 cups ice cubes
1 tablespoon hempseed oil
1 teaspoon pure vanilla extract
Grated zest of ½ fresh lemon (1 to 1½ teaspoons)

Place all the ingredients in a food processor or blender and purée until smooth and creamy.

This smoothie is a great way to get your omega essential fatty acids. It tastes like the richest milkshake imaginable.

Cool Gruel

Makes 2 to 3 servings

¼ cup shelled hempseed
2 cups spring or filtered water
1 medium Granny Smith apple, cored and diced (do not peel)
1 cup rolled oats
Pinch of ground cinnamon
Pinch of sea salt

Place a dry skillet over medium-low heat. When hot, add the hempseed and toast, stirring constantly, for 2 minutes or until fragrant.

Combine the water, apple, oats, cinnamon, and salt in a saucepan. Simmer over medium-low heat, stirring frequently, for 5 to 7 minutes or until all the liquid is absorbed and the oats are creamy. Remove from the heat and stir in the toasted hempseed. Spoon into individual cereal bowls and serve hot.

Variations:

• Add organic raisins or other dried fruit of your choice.

• For a richer cereal, use vanilla soymilk in place of the water.

• For a sweeter cereal, stir in 1 to 2 tablespoons of brown rice syrup just before serving.

Beginning your day with this powerfully nutritious porridge will give you energy to burn.

Stone-Ground Grits

Makes 2 to 3 servings

2½ cups spring or filtered water
½ cup yellow corn grits
¼ cup fresh or frozen corn kernels
Generous pinch of sea salt
1 tablespoon shelled hempseed
1 to 2 teaspoons extra-virgin olive oil
2 to 3 sprigs fresh parsley, minced (for garnish)

Place the water in a saucepan and whisk in the corn grits, corn, and salt. Place over medium heat and bring to a boil, whisking constantly. When the mixture boils, reduce the heat to low and cook, stirring frequently, until the center bubbles and pops, about 25 minutes.

Remove from the heat and whisk in the hempseed and olive oil. Serve immediately, garnished with the parsley.

I love this porridge on warm summer mornings when I want a light breakfast. Sunny yellow corn grits join forces with nutritious hempseed to create a nutty, delicious way to start any day.

Sweet Morning Polenta

2½ cups vanilla soymilk or rice milk
½ cup yellow corn grits
¼ cup golden raisins
Generous pinch of sea salt
1 tablespoon shelled hempseed
1 to 2 teaspoons slivered almonds (for garnish)

Place the soymilk in a saucepan and whisk in the corn grits, raisins, and salt. Place over medium heat and bring to a boil, whisking constantly. When the mixture boils, reduce the heat to low and cook, stirring frequently, until the center bubbles and pops, about 25 minutes.

Remove from the heat and whisk in the hempseed. Serve garnished with the slivered almonds.

Variation: When in season, garnish with fresh berries in addition to or in place of the almonds.

Enjoy this version of soft polenta whenever you want a sweet start to the day.

Quick Whole Grain Porridge

Makes 3 to 4 servings

2 to 3 cups vanilla soymilk or apple juice
1 cup cooked grain (such as rice, millet, barley, or whole oats)
⅓ cup organic raisins
Generous pinch of ground cinnamon
Pinch of sea salt
1 to 2 tablespoons shelled hempseed

Combine the soymilk, cooked grain, raisins, cinnamon, and salt in a saucepan over medium heat. Cover and bring to a boil. Reduce the heat to low and cook 15 to 20 minutes or until all the liquid has been absorbed and the grain is creamy.

Place a dry skillet over medium heat. When the skillet is hot, add the hempseed and toast, stirring constantly, until fragrant, about 2 minutes. Stir into the porridge just before serving.

Wondering what to do with the leftover grain from dinner? Try this delicately sweet morning porridge. With the power of whole grains and hempseed, you'll be energized all day long.

Scrambled Tofu
with Herb-Scented Hempseed

Makes 4 to 5 servings

Extra-virgin olive oil
1 red onion, sliced into thin half-moons
Sea salt
Generous pinch of turmeric
4 to 5 button mushrooms, brushed free of dirt and thinly sliced
1 carrot, cut into fine matchsticks
⅔ cup fresh or frozen corn kernels
1 pound extra-firm tofu, coarsely crumbled
2 tablespoons Herb-Scented Hempseed, page 75
3 to 4 sprigs fresh parsley, minced

Place a small amount of olive oil in a skillet. Add the onion and place over medium heat. When the onion begins to sizzle, add a pinch of salt and turmeric and sauté for 2 minutes. Stir in the mushrooms and carrot and a pinch more salt. Sauté for 2 minutes. Stir in the corn. Crumble the tofu into the skillet and stir well. Add 1 or 2 tablespoons of water, season to taste with salt, cover, and cook over low heat 3 to 4 minutes or until the liquid is absorbed. Stir in the hempseed and parsley. Serve hot.

Need a bit of protein in the morning to keep your energy high? Rather than hard-to-digest bacon or eggs, try this delicately-flavored tofu dish. Trust me, no one will miss omelets.

Granola

Makes 5 to 6 cups

¼ cup light-colored olive or avocado oil
¼ cup brown rice syrup or pure maple syrup
1½ teaspoons pure vanilla extract
Grated zest of 1 fresh orange (about 1½ tablespoons)
Pinch of sea salt
Pinch of ground cinnamon
4 cups rolled oats
½ cup raw sunflower seeds
½ cup raw pumpkin seeds
½ cup slivered almonds
½ cup shelled hempseed

Preheat the oven to 350°F and line a baking sheet with parchment.

Combine the oil, syrup, vanilla extract, orange zest, salt, and cinnamon in a small bowl and whisk until well combined. Place the oats, sunflower seeds, pumpkin seeds, almonds, and hempseed in a large bowl. Pour the wet ingredients over the dry ingredients and mix well to coat evenly. Spread as thinly as possible on the lined baking sheet. Bake until the almonds are lightly browned, about 20 minutes. Remove from the oven and cool completely. Stir well to combine. Transfer to a tightly sealed container and store in the refrigerator for one to two weeks.

Variation: Add 1 cup coarsely chopped dried fruit after the granola has finished baking. Good choices are organic raisins, apples, prunes, dates, or apricots.

I know what you're thinking: Oh, here it is, the granola recipe. Well, this isn't just any old granola. Give it a try—you'll love it!

Muesli

2 cups rolled oats
1 cup shelled hempseed
½ cup coarsely chopped pecans
½ cup raw pumpkin seeds
½ cup unsweetened shredded coconut
Pinch of sea salt
½ cup chopped dried apricots
½ cup organic raisins

Preheat the oven to 325°F and line a baking sheet with parchment.

Combine the oats, hempseed, pecans, pumpkin seeds, coconut, and salt in a large bowl. Spread on the prepared baking sheet and bake briefly, just for 7 to 10 minutes. Remove from the oven and let cool completely. Transfer to a mixing bowl and stir in the dried fruit. Store in an airtight container in a cool place.

Muesli is a lovely European version of granola—sort of a sophisticated twist on an old hippie recipe. It's great as a snack, morning cereal, or dessert topping.

Waffles

¾ cup whole wheat pastry flour
¾ cup yellow cornmeal
1 teaspoon shelled hempseed
1 teaspoon aluminum-free baking powder
Pinch of sea salt
3 ounces silken tofu
1 to 2 tablespoons light-colored olive oil
2 teaspoons brown rice syrup
1 teaspoon pure vanilla extract
Splash of umeboshi vinegar
½ to 1 cup vanilla soymilk

Place the flour, cornmeal, hempseed, baking powder, and salt in a bowl and stir with a dry whisk until well combined. Place the tofu, olive oil, rice syrup, vanilla extract, and vinegar in a blender and purée until smooth. Fold into the flour mixture. Slowly stir in the soymilk to form a thick batter.

Preheat a well-oiled waffle iron. When the iron is hot, spoon 2 to 3 tablespoons of batter onto the iron and close. Cook 3 to 4 minutes or until firm. Place on a baking sheet and keep warm in a slow oven while you make the rest of the waffles. Serve topped with maple syrup, Fruit Compote, page 54, or sliced fresh berries.

Nothing says "this breakfast is special" quite like waffles. For a lazy Sunday or leisurely brunch with those you love most, enjoy these anytime you'd like a delicious treat to start your day.

Fruit Compote

1 ripe apple, cored and diced (do not peel)
1 firm, ripe pear, cored and diced (do not peel)
2 to 3 tablespoons vanilla soymilk or rice milk
2 tablespoons organic raisins
Grated zest of 1 fresh lemon (2 to 3 teaspoons)
1 to 2 teaspoons brown rice syrup
1 teaspoon pure vanilla extract
Pinch of sea salt
Pinch of ground cinnamon
2 teaspoons shelled hempseed
2 teaspoons unsweetened shredded coconut

Combine the apple, pear, soymilk, raisins, lemon zest, rice syrup, vanilla extract, salt, and cinnamon in a saucepan and place over medium-low heat. Cover and cook 20 to 25 minutes or until the apple and pear are tender. Uncover and simmer until any remaining liquid has been absorbed. Serve topped with the hempseed and coconut.

Variation: Choose seasonal fruit for various compotes. Fresh berries and peaches will require far less cooking time (usually 7 to 10 minutes) than denser fruit, such as apples and pears. Note that cinnamon may not work well with every fruit, so you may choose to omit it.

This is a great topping for waffles or pancakes. It also makes a light, special occasion breakfast treat.

Pancakes

Makes about 10 pancakes

1 cup whole wheat pastry flour
1 teaspoon aluminum-free baking powder
Pinch of sea salt
¾ to 1 cup vanilla soymilk or rice milk
1 tablespoon light-colored olive oil or avocado oil
1 teaspoon umeboshi vinegar
2 teaspoons shelled hempseed

Combine the flour, baking powder, and salt in a large bowl. Stir with a dry whisk for about 1 minute. In a separate bowl, combine the soymilk, olive oil, and vinegar, and whisk until well blended. Pour into the flour mixture and whisk briskly for 1 minute, adding a little more soymilk if the mixture seems too thick. Fold in the hempseed.

Lightly oil a griddle or skillet with a little olive oil and warm over medium heat. Using about ¼ cup of the batter per pancake, spoon onto the hot griddle and cook until golden on both sides, turning once. Serve with Fruit Compote, page 54, pure maple syrup, or unsweetened fruit preserves.

Variation: To create different versions of the basic pancake recipe, use ¾ cup whole wheat pastry flour with ¼ cup spelt flour, cornmeal, or buckwheat flour.

For me, it's not Sunday morning without a plate of these light-as-air pancakes. So easy, so delicious, so wonderful—you won't want a weekend to pass without them.

French Toast

1 cup vanilla soymilk
1 tablespoon brown rice syrup
1 teaspoon hempseed oil
1 tablespoon whole wheat pastry flour
1 tablespoon semolina flour
½ teaspoon aluminum-free baking powder
Pinch of sea salt
2 tablespoons shelled hempseed, ground into a fine meal
Light-colored olive oil or avocado oil
4 to 6 thick slices whole grain sourdough bread

Combine the soymilk, rice syrup, and hempseed oil in a large bowl. Whisk in the flours, baking powder, and salt, beating until smooth. Fold in the hempseed meal.

Place enough olive oil in a skillet to coat the bottom and place over medium heat. Dip 1 slice of the bread into the batter and pan fry each side until golden. Repeat with the remaining batter and bread. Serve with pure maple syrup and fresh, seasonal berries.

Note: To grind the hempseed, place it in a blender and pulse to create a fine meal.

I used to think that an egg-free diet meant no more French toast. Was I wrong! Ground hempseed helps the batter adhere to the bread because it's more than 30 percent albumin-like protein. How sweet it is!

Supersonic Tonic Breakfast

Makes 1 to 2 servings

1 cup plain soy yogurt
½ cup fresh or thawed frozen blueberries or other berries
½ cup shelled hempseed
½ ripe banana, sliced
Grated zest of 1 fresh orange (about 1½ tablespoons)
1 tablespoon lecithin granules
1 tablespoon hempseed oil
¼ teaspoon bee pollen (optional)

Place the soy yogurt in a bowl and fold in the berries, hempseed, banana, orange zest, lecithin granules, hempseed oil, and optional bee pollen. Mix gently to combine. Serve at room temperature or chilled.

This is a great way to kick-start your engines on those mornings when there's just no time to cook. It doesn't get any easier than this!

dips and sandwich spreads

From peanut butter to more exotic dips and spreads, hempseed adds a depth of flavor that takes any recipe to new heights. High in fiber, over 30 percent complete protein, rich in essential fatty acids, and a good source of vitamins and minerals, hempseed gives us so many nutrients it will make you want to throw a party to celebrate. With these recipe options, you can host a wonderful bash knowing that the food you're serving is as healthful for your guests as it is delicious.

—Christina

Hummus

Makes about 4 cups

1-inch piece kombu
1½ cups dried chickpeas, sorted, rinsed, and soaked for 1 hour
5 cups spring or filtered water
½ cup sesame tahini
Juice of 1 fresh lemon (about 3 tablespoons)
1 to 2 teaspoons sea salt
2 cloves fresh garlic, thinly sliced
¼ cup shelled hempseed
2 to 3 sprigs fresh parsley, minced
2 teaspoons minced fresh mint

Place the kombu in the bottom of a pressure cooker. Drain the chickpeas and place them on top of the kombu. Add the water and bring to a rolling boil. Lock the lid in place and bring to full pressure. Reduce the heat to low and cook for 55 minutes. Remove from the heat and allow the pressure to come down naturally.

Drain the chickpeas (reserving some of the cooking water) and transfer to a food processor. Add the tahini, lemon juice, salt to taste, and garlic and purée until smooth, slowly adding just enough of the cooking water to create a creamy texture. Adjust the seasonings to your taste and purée again. Transfer to a serving bowl and fold in the hempseed, parsley, and mint. Serve warm or chilled, with raw vegetable sticks, pita bread, or organic corn chips.

Note: If you don't have a pressure cooker, you can cook the chickpeas in a heavy pot for 1 to 2 hours or until soft. Alternatively, you may use canned organic chickpeas (about 2¾ cups or two 15-ounce cans) to save time, but rinse them very well before puréeing.

This traditional Middle Eastern chickpea dip gets a powerful boost of nutrients with the addition of hempseed. Creamy and rich, it is fabulous for parties, lunches, and snacks.

Guacamole

2 large, ripe avocados
2 tablespoons fresh lime or lemon juice
2 medium tomatoes, cut into small dice
½ cup minced shallots or red onion
1 clove fresh garlic, minced
¼ cup shelled hempseed
½ to ⅔ teaspoon sea salt
1 to 2 teaspoons minced fresh cilantro (optional)
Generous pinch of chili powder (optional)

Peel the avocados and place them in a bowl with the lime juice. Using a fork, mash until smooth. Fold in the tomatoes, shallots, and garlic until well incorporated. Fold in the hempseed, salt to taste, and optional cilantro and chili powder. Serve with raw vegetable sticks, chips, or crackers, or use as a sandwich spread.

No party is complete without this creamy, decadent dip. Mashed avocados are blended with the gentle bite of shallots, the lively freshness of tomatoes, and the tang of lime juice to create the perfect symphony of flavors.

Tofu Skinny Dip

Makes 1 to 2 cups

1 pound extra-firm tofu, boiled for 5 minutes and drained
    (see note below)
2 tablespoons sweet white miso
2 tablespoons fresh lemon juice
2 tablespoons extra-virgin olive oil
2 to 3 shallots, minced
1 to 2 cloves fresh garlic, minced
3 tablespoons pine nuts
2 tablespoons minced fresh basil, or 1 teaspoon dried basil
3 tablespoons shelled hempseed
3 tablespoons minced oil-cured black olives
½ red bell pepper, roasted over an open flame, peeled,
    seeded, and diced (see page 63)

Crumble the tofu and place it in a food processor along with the miso and lemon juice. Purée until smooth.

Place the oil in a skillet. Add the shallots and garlic in a skillet and place over medium heat. When the shallots begin to sizzle, sauté for 1 minute. Do not burn the garlic. Stir in the pine nuts and basil. Spoon the sautéed vegetables into the tofu mixture in the food processor and purée until smooth. Transfer to a mixing bowl and fold in the hempseed, olives, and red pepper. Serve with raw vegetable slices, chips, or crackers, or use as a sandwich spread.

Note: Boiling the tofu for 5 minutes aids in digestion, creates a creamier spread, and minimizes the "beany" flavor of tofu that can overpower the other flavors in the dip.

Low in fat and high in protein and essential fatty acids, this festive dip is rich and delicious.

Lentil Pâté

2 cups cooked brown or green lentils

Extra-virgin olive oil

1 red onion, finely diced

1 to 2 cloves garlic, minced

Sea salt

Pepper

Generous pinch of crushed red pepper flakes

1 carrot, finely diced

2 to 3 tablespoons dry white wine

¼ cup sesame tahini

¼ cup pan toasted shelled hempseed (see page 44)

1 red bell pepper, roasted over an open flame and peeled, seeded, and
   diced (see note page 63)

Drain the lentils and cool completely. Place a generous amount of oil in a skillet. Add the onion and garlic and place over medium heat. When the onion begins to sizzle, add a pinch of salt, pepper, and red pepper flakes to taste and sauté for 1 to 2 minutes. Stir in the carrot and another pinch of salt and sauté 1 minute. Add the wine, season to taste with salt and pepper, and reduce the heat to low. Simmer until the carrot is tender, about 5 minutes.

Combine the cooked lentils, sautéed vegetables, and tahini in a food processor and purée until smooth. Transfer to a bowl and fold in the hempseed and roasted red pepper. Serve with raw vegetable slices, chips, or crackers, or use as a sandwich spread.

A creamy pâté adds a touch of elegance to just about any occasion. Our version, rich in protein and essential fatty acids, is as scrumptious as it is good for you. It makes a great starter course or party food.

Mango Salsa

Makes 2 to 3 cups

2 cups diced ripe mangoes
½ red onion, finely diced
½ cup minced fresh cilantro
¼ cup shelled hempseed
Juice of 1 fresh lime or lemon (2 to 3 tablespoons)
1 tablespoon brown rice syrup
1 tablespoon extra-virgin olive oil
2 teaspoons minced fresh ginger
Sea salt
Pepper
Pinch of cayenne pepper
Pinch of chili powder

Combine all the ingredients in a bowl. Adjust the seasonings to taste and gently toss to incorporate the flavors throughout. Cover and refrigerate for 2 hours before serving to develop the flavors.

This salsa is sweet and spicy, just like the perfect date. We marry the sweet flesh of mango with peppery onions and hot spices. It's the ideal dipping sauce for vegetables, chips, or fried tempeh.

Note: To roast a pepper, place a clean, raw pepper directly on a burner and turn the flame to high. Char the outer skin completely, turning the pepper to ensure even charring. Transfer the blackened pepper to a paper sack, seal tightly, and allow the pepper to steam for 10 minutes. Remove the pepper from the sack and gently rub off the charred skin with your fingers. Carefully rinse any remaining black residue from the pepper. Alternatively, you may roast the pepper under the broiler. Slice it in half lengthwise and put it cut-side down on a baking sheet. Place under the broiler until charred.

Winter Squash Spread

2 cups diced winter squash, peeled and seeded
　　(good choices are acorn, butternut, or hokkaido)
Extra-virgin olive oil
Barley malt
Sea salt
Generous pinch of ground cinnamon
Scant pinch of grated nutmeg
¼ cup shelled hempseed

Preheat the oven to 350°F and lightly oil a 9 x 13-inch baking dish.

Place the squash cubes in a mixing bowl and drizzle generously with the oil and barley malt. Season lightly with the salt, cinnamon, and nutmeg. Toss gently to coat. Spread the seasoned squash cubes in the prepared baking dish and cover tightly with foil. Bake 45 to 60 minutes or until the squash is quite soft. Remove from the oven and let cool completely.

Place the cooked squash in a food processor and purée until smooth. Transfer to a bowl and fold in the hempseed.

This is the best cold-weather spread imaginable. I love it on muffins, cornbread, or simple morning toast. Give it a try—you'll love it, too.

HempNut Butter

Makes about 2 cups

1 cup organic crunchy peanut butter
¼ cup shelled hempseed
1 tablespoon extra-virgin olive oil or hempseed oil
1 tablespoon spring or filtered water
Sea salt

Place the peanut butter in a small bowl. Place the hempseed in a dry skillet over medium heat and toast, stirring constantly, until fragrant, about 2 minutes. Set aside to cool. Transfer the hempseed to a blender or food processor and pulse to create a fine meal. Stir into the peanut butter along with the olive oil, water, and salt to taste. Using a fork, mix until smooth. Transfer to a jar and store in a cool place.

Packed with protein, this creamy dip is perfect to serve with celery sticks or whole grain crackers. It's so delicious, there's no excuse for not eating well!

Creamy Almond Spread

Makes 1 to 2 cups

1 cup creamy almond butter
½ cup shelled hempseed
1 tablespoon sweet white miso
1 teaspoon brown rice syrup
Juice of 1 fresh lemon (about 3 tablespoons)
Spring or filtered water

Combine the almond butter, hempseed, miso, and rice syrup in a bowl. Stir until thoroughly mixed. It will be quite stiff. Stir in the lemon juice. Slowly stir in just enough water to achieve a creamy, spreadable consistency.

This creamy, savory spread is ideal for morning toast when you don't want a sweet spread sending your blood sugar off the charts. It's also a great afternoon pick-me-up, a satisfying treat with high protein and essential fatty acids.

Black Bean Salsa

½ cup dried black beans, rinsed well and soaked for 1 hour

2 cups spring or filtered water

2 fresh red Fresno chilies

1 poblano chili

1 red onion, diced

Grated zest and juice of 1 lime (about 1 teaspoon zest;
    1 to 2 tablespoons juice)

2 tablespoons dark beer

2 tablespoons shelled hempseed, lightly pan toasted (see page 44)

3 to 4 sprigs fresh cilantro, minced

1 tablespoon extra-virgin olive oil

Sea salt

Drain the beans and place them in a heavy saucepan. Add the water and bring to a boil. Reduce the heat to low, cover, and cook until the beans are tender, about 45 minutes. Drain and rinse well. Set aside to cool.

Spear the chilies with skewers and char them over an open flame. If you do not have a gas range, split the chilies, leaving the seeds inside. Arrange them them on a baking sheet, cut-side down and place under the broiler until the skin is charred. Place the chilies in a paper sack and set aside for 10 minutes to steam and loosen the skin. Remove the skins using your fingers and scrape out the seeds. Finely mince.

Combine the cooked beans, roasted chilies, red onion, lime zest and juice, beer, hempseed, cilantro, olive oil, and salt to taste. Mix well and chill thoroughly. Serve with tortilla chips.

Note: Two (15- or 16-ounce) cans of organic black beans may be used in place of the dried beans.

Here's a slightly spicy, richly flavored salsa that will add life to any feast or party.

Roasted Tomato Salsa

Makes 5 to 6 servings

10 to 12 plum tomatoes, quartered lengthwise

8 whole shallots, peeled

5 whole cloves fresh garlic, peeled

Sea salt

2 dried poblano chilies

Grated zest and juice of 1 fresh lemon (2 to 3 teaspoons zest; about 3 tablespoons juice)

2 tablespoons extra-virgin olive oil

1 tablespoon shelled hempseed, lightly pan toasted (see page 44)

1 teaspoon brown rice syrup

1 sprig fresh rosemary, leaves stripped

Preheat the oven to 325°F. Arrange the tomato pieces on a baking sheet. Arrange the shallots and garlic among the tomatoes. Sprinkle with salt. Roast until beginning to dry, about 1½ hours. Do not let the vegetables burn or blacken. Cool the tomatoes and peel. Mince the tomatoes, shallots, and garlic. Transfer to a bowl.

Soak the chilies in very hot water for 10 minutes. Drain and remove the stems. Split lengthwise, remove the seeds, and mince.

Stir the chilies, lemon zest and juice, olive oil, hempseed, rice syrup, rosemary leaves, and salt to taste into the tomato mixture. Mix well and allow to stand for about 1 hour before serving. Serve at room temperature or chilled, with tortilla chips.

There's ordinary tomato salsa and then there's phenomenal tomato salsa. Once you try this version, you'll never turn back.

sauces

If you think sauce means marinara out of a jar, think again. A natural sauce is the sensual, sexy touch that can take a dish from the simple to the sublime. The most humble vegetable or the simplest salad literally sparkles when just the right sauce caresses it. Like a gentle lover, sauces coax and woo a dish, lifting flavors to delightful new heights.

Sauces enchant simple pasta dishes, coat vegetables with silky richness, and lift mild-mannered grains to superhero status. So be a bit saucy!

—Christina

condiments

Condiments are spectacular vehicles for balancing the taste and energy of various dishes and meals. Want a bit more flavor? Need a tad more saltiness? Crave just a smidge more richness? Condiments allow us to balance the taste of our food exactly as we desire. Using hempseed in our condiments makes our foods super nutritious as well.

—Christina

Pesto

Makes 1 to 2 cups

8 to 10 stalks fresh basil, washed, drained, leaves removed
5 cloves fresh garlic, thinly sliced
½ cup pine nuts or walnut pieces
¼ cup shelled hempseed
1 tablespoon sweet white miso
¼ cup extra-virgin olive oil
¼ cup hempseed oil
1 teaspoon umeboshi vinegar
1 teaspoon brown rice syrup

Place the basil leaves and garlic in a food processor and pulse to create a coarse paste. Add the pine nuts, hempseed, and miso and pulse until evenly combined. Add the olive oil, hempseed oil, vinegar, and rice syrup and purée until smooth. Adjust the seasonings to suit your taste.

Slowly add a small amount of water, only if desired to create a thinner consistency. Do not thin the pesto too much or it won't cling to the pasta. Toss with freshly cooked pasta or serve with fresh vegetables as a dip.

Note: If you prefer to make the pesto in advance but want to retain the bright green color, briefly dip the fresh basil leaves in boiling water and drain them well before continuing with the recipe.

When summer is at its peak and the garden is lush with fragrant basil, can you think of anything besides silky pasta, smothered in sensual pesto? Me, either.

Caramelized Onion Gravy

Makes about 2 cups

1 yellow onion, cut into thin half-moons
1 tablespoon hempseed oil
1 to 2 cloves fresh garlic, minced
Natural soy sauce
2 cups spring or filtered water
2 teaspoons kuzu, dissolved in 2 tablespoons cold
    spring or filtered water

Combine the onion and oil in a small saucepan and place over medium heat. Sauté until the onion starts to brown, as long as 15 minutes. (Do not add water, as the onion will not brown as well.)

Stir in the garlic and sauté 1 minute. Season lightly with soy sauce and add the water. Cover and bring to a boil. Reduce the heat to low and season to taste with soy sauce. Cook for 7 minutes. Stir in the dissolved kuzu and cook, stirring constantly, until the gravy thickens and clears, about 3 minutes.

Sometimes the simplest dish can come to life with a rich, savory gravy. Well, here's a basic recipe that's perfect for everyday meals as well as the sublimely fancy.

Gomasio

Makes 1 generous cup

3 tablespoons sea salt
1 cup shelled hempseed

Place a dry skillet over medium-low heat. When the pan is hot, dry roast the salt until the strong aroma has dissipated. Stir in the hempseed and cook, stirring constantly, 2 to 3 minutes or until the seeds are toasted. Take care that they do not burn. Transfer to a bowl and allow to cool completely. Store in a tightly sealed glass jar in a cool, dry place.

This is like rocket fuel—roasted salt carries nutrients deep into our bodies so the hempseed's complete protein and essential fatty acids are used efficiently to keep us healthy and strong. Serve on grains, pasta, and vegetables.

Lemony HempNut Sauce

Makes about 1½ cups

1 cup sesame tahini
2 to 3 scallions, minced
¼ cup fresh lemon juice
2 tablespoons shelled hempseed
1 tablespoon umeboshi vinegar
2 teaspoons brown rice syrup
2 cloves fresh garlic, minced
Sea salt
Generous pinch of ground cumin

Place all the ingredients in a mortar and pestle, suribachi (grinding bowl), or blender. Purée until smooth. Adjust the seasonings to taste.

Note: While it may be a bit more work, the sauce will turn out best when puréed by hand in a suribachi. The grinding releases the oils in the hempseed and the juices in the scallions to create a depth of flavor that can't be achieved in a blender.

This rich, creamy sauce will add sparkle to any simple dish. Try it over steamed greens or fresh salad, or keep it sensually thick and serve it as a dip for falafel or raw vegetables.

HempNut Cream

Makes about 2 cups

2 cups plain amasake or vanilla soymilk
2 tablespoons shelled hempseed, ground into a fine meal (see note below)
1 tablespoon brown rice syrup
1 teaspoon pure vanilla extract
Pinch of sea salt
Scant pinch of ground cinnamon (optional)
3 tablespoons arrowroot or kuzu

Combine the amasake, ground hempseed, rice syrup, vanilla extract, salt, and optional cinnamon in a small saucepan over medium-low heat. When the mixture is warmed through, dissolve the arrowroot in a small amount of cold water and stir into the warm liquid. Cook, stirring constantly, until the mixture thickens and turns creamy, 3 to 4 minutes. Transfer to a heat-resistant bowl and cover tightly with plastic (to prevent a "skin" from forming). Chill completely. Prior to using, whisk to loosen and smooth. Dollop over fresh fruit, compotes, cobblers, cakes, or puddings.

Note: To grind hempseed, simply place a tablespoon in a coffee or spice grinder and pulse to create a fine meal.

Do you want to give up dairy but the thought of life without whipped cream is just too much? Well, this isn't Cool Whip, but it's creamy and sweet and will satisfy your cravings without compromising your health.

Raita

2 ripe bananas

3 cups unsweetened plain soy yogurt

3 tablespoons shelled hempseed, ground into a
    fine meal (see page 56)

3 tablespoons brown rice syrup

½ teaspoon ground coriander

½ teaspoon ground cumin

½ teaspoon ground cinnamon

There's a bit of tropical sweetness in this creamy, decadent pudding sauce. The savory spices add just a touch of exotic flair. Try a few dollops over pancakes or waffles.

Place the bananas in a bowl and mash them with a fork to create a smooth paste. Fold in the yogurt, hempseed, and rice syrup. Mix well. Fold in the spices, adjusting the flavors to suit your taste.

Garlic Butter

⅓ cup shelled hempseed

2 tablespoons hempseed oil

2 tablespoons extra-virgin olive oil

4 to 5 sprigs fresh parsley, finely minced

4 cloves garlic, peeled and minced

Grated zest of 1 lemon (2 to 3 teaspoons)

Generous pinch of sea salt

Combine all the ingredients in a suribachi (grinding bowl) or mortar and pestle. Purée until somewhat creamy but not completely smooth. Alternatively, pulse the ingredients in a blender or food processor to create a coarse but creamy texture. This spread will keep for about one week stored in the refrigerator.

Having a hard time giving up butter? Not any more! This decadently rich, garlicky spread will win raves, and no one will miss slathering saturated fat or hydrogenated oil on their bread.

Spiced HempNut

Makes 1 cup

1 cup shelled hempseed
1 teaspoon natural soy sauce
Generous pinch of ground coriander
Generous pinch of powdered ginger

Place a dry skillet over medium-low heat and stir in the hempseed and soy sauce. Lightly pan toast the hempseed, stirring constantly for 1 minute. Add the spices and pan toast until fragrant, about 2 minutes longer. Transfer to a glass jar and cool completely before sealing. This condiment will keep for 2 to 3 weeks stored in a cool, dry place.

This nutty condiment is perfect for sprinkling on grains and vegetables, taking them from simple to sublime. Just a touch of this spice showcases the naturally rich flavor of the hempseed.

Curried Hempseed

Makes about ⅓ cup

1 teaspoon curry powder
Generous pinch of sea salt
¼ cup shelled hempseed

Place a dry skillet over medium heat until warmed. Stir in the curry powder and salt and pan toast them for 2 to 3 minutes. Stir in the hempseed and toast, stirring constantly, for 2 to 3 minutes or until the seeds are fragrant. Take care not to burn the seeds. Transfer to a glass jar and cool completely before sealing. This condiment will keep for 1 to 2 weeks stored in a cool, dry place.

Delicately spicy, this condiment adds just the right touch of sassiness to any vegetable, grain, or bean dish.

Herb-Scented Hempseed

Makes about ⅓ cup

1 teaspoon sea salt
2 teaspoons dried basil
2 teaspoons dried thyme
¼ cup shelled hempseed

Place a dry skillet over medium heat. When the skillet is hot, dry roast the salt for 1 to 2 minutes. Stir in the dried herbs and roast them for 2 minutes. Stir in the hempseed and pan toast it for 3 to 4 minutes. Transfer to a glass jar and cool completely before sealing. This condiment will keep for 1 to 2 weeks stored in a cool, dry place.

I love this condiment sprinkled on simple grain dishes. But my favorite? I cook pasta with olive oil and garlic and sprinkle these flavorful seeds over the top.

Asian-Spiced Hempseed

Makes about ½ cup

¼ cup shelled hempseed
1 tablespoon natural soy sauce
1 teaspoon chili powder

Combine the hempseed, soy sauce, and chili powder in a dry skillet and place over medium-low heat. Pan toast, stirring constantly, for 2 to 3 minutes or until the hempseed is quite fragrant. Transfer to a glass jar and cool completely before sealing. This condiment will keep 1 to 2 weeks stored in a cool, dry place.

This spicy, salty condiment will make your grain dishes sparkle. As it is strongly flavored, just a light sprinkle will do the job.

soups

Regardless of the season, no meal is complete without soup. Sensual, warming, and relaxing, soup is more than just delicious broth.

Ever wonder why soup is the starter course of a meal? Soup is warm liquid, soothing and comforting. As the beginning of a meal, soup helps to relax the digestive system, aiding in the efficient assimilation of the nutrients in the meal to follow.

Soup also sets the tone of the meal. A simple consommé, with delicate pieces of vegetables floating elegantly in a light broth, is an indication that the meal to follow will be rich and hearty. A richly flavored soup, thick with grains or beans and vegetables, is almost a feast in itself and indicates that the remainder of the meal will be light and fresh.

Soup relaxes us, warms us, and works as a great vehicle for transporting nutrients deep into our bodies. That's one of the reasons that soup leaves us feeling completely nourished. Adding shelled hempseed or hempseed oil to soup makes it even better. So make a bowl of soup, sit down, and enjoy.

—Christina

Sweet Potato Corn Soup

Makes 4 to 5 servings

Extra-virgin olive oil
1 yellow onion, finely diced
2 cloves fresh garlic, minced
2 teaspoons curry or chili powder
Sea salt
2 teaspoons mirin
2 medium sweet potatoes, peeled and diced
4 cups plain soymilk
2 cups fresh or frozen corn kernels
Shelled hempseed, lightly pan toasted (see page 44)
2 to 3 sprigs fresh cilantro or basil, minced
4 to 5 slices fresh lime

Place a small amount of oil in a soup pot. Add the onion and garlic and place over medium heat. When the onion begins to sizzle, add the curry powder and a pinch of salt. Sauté for 2 to 3 minutes. Add the mirin and simmer for 2 to 3 minutes. Stir in the sweet potatoes and sauté for 1 to 2 minutes. Add the soymilk, cover, and bring to a boil. Reduce the heat to low and cook until the sweet potatoes are quite soft, about 25 minutes.

Transfer to a food processor and purée until smooth. Return to the soup pot and place over low heat. Season to taste with salt and stir in the corn. Simmer for 3 to 4 minutes. Serve garnished with the hempseed, cilantro, and a slice of lime in each bowl.

The married flavors of sweet potato and corn are so delicious they can make us swoon. Both earthy and sunny, these hearty ingredients come together to make the perfect winter weather soup.

Beet Borscht

Borscht:

Extra virgin olive oil
1 yellow onion, diced
Sea salt
3 medium Yukon Gold potatoes, peeled and diced
1 cup diced cabbage
6 medium beets, peeled and diced
6 cups spring or filtered water or plain soymilk
¼ cup shelled hempseed

Tofu Sour Cream:

4 ounces silken tofu
1 teaspoon brown rice syrup
Splash umeboshi vinegar
Sea salt
2 to 3 sprigs fresh parsley, minced (for garnish)

Place a small amount of oil in a soup pot. Add the onion and place over medium heat. When the onion begins to sizzle, add a pinch of salt and sauté for 2 to 3 minutes. Stir in the potatoes and cabbage, add a pinch of salt, and sauté for 1 to 2 minutes. Stir in the beets and sauté until just shiny with oil. Add the water, cover, and bring to a boil. Reduce the heat to low and cook until the beets are soft, about 25 minutes. Stir in the hempseed. Transfer to a food processor and purée until smooth. Return to the soup pot and place over low heat. Season to taste with salt and simmer for 5 to 7 minutes.

While the soup cooks, prepare the tofu sour cream. Combine the tofu, rice syrup, vinegar, and salt to taste in a food processor and

Borscht is a traditional vegetable soup, delicately sweet and incredibly nourishing. High in potassium, magnesium, and essential fatty acids, this warming soup is a great way to start any meal.

purée until creamy. Transfer to a small bowl, cover, and chill thoroughly. To serve, spoon the soup into individual bowls, place a dollop of tofu sour cream in the center, and sprinkle with the parsley.

Gazpacho

Makes 3 to 4 servings

3 ripe tomatoes, diced
½ cup tomato juice
1 small yellow onion, diced
1 green bell pepper, diced
¼ cup fresh lemon or lime juice
3 to 4 sprigs fresh basil, leaves removed
1 clove fresh garlic, thinly sliced
Sea salt
½ cup shelled hempseed
½ small cucumber, thinly sliced into rounds

Combine the tomatoes, tomato juice, onion, bell pepper, lemon juice, basil leaves, and garlic in a food processor and purée until smooth. Season to taste with salt and purée again. Chill thoroughly. To serve, spoon the soup into individual bowls and sprinkle with the hempseed and cucumber slices. If the gazpacho seems too thick, add a small amount of cold water.

Variation: For a chunky gazpacho, do not purée the bell pepper. Instead, stir it into the blended soup.

When summer is sizzling hot and you feel as wilted as week-old daisies, try this chilled, refreshing soup that will cool you down quickly. It features summer's brightest stars: fresh, juicy tomatoes and peppers.

Shiitake Mushroom Barley Soup

Makes 7 to 8 servings

1 tablespoon extra-virgin olive oil

1 yellow onion, diced

2 cloves fresh garlic, minced

Sea salt

1½ cups dried shiitake mushrooms, soaked until tender,
    drained, and thinly sliced

3 cups plain soymilk

2 cups spring or filtered water

1 cups pearl barley, rinsed very well

1½ tablespoons sweet white miso

1 tablespoon hempseed oil

½ cup shelled hempseed

2 to 3 sprigs fresh parsley, minced

Place the oil in a soup pot. Add the onion and garlic and place over medium heat. When the onion begins to sizzle, add a pinch of salt and sauté for 1 to 2 minutes. Do not brown the onions. Stir in the shiitake mushrooms and sauté just until coated with oil. Add the soymilk, water, and barley. Cover and bring to a boil. Reduce the heat to low and cook until the barley is quite soft and creamy, about 35 minutes.

Remove a few tablespoons of the broth and combine it with the miso. Pour the miso mixture into the soup, stir in the hempseed oil, and cook for 3 to 4 minutes. To serve, spoon the soup into individual bowls and garnish with the hempseed and parsley.

Mushroom soup is creamy, rich, and comforting—who doesn't love it? This soup is not only a delicious starter course for any meal, it has the cleansing energy of shiitake mushrooms, which keep the soup light, and the added nutrient boost of shelled hempseed and oil.

Carrot Ginger Soup

Makes 6 to 8 servings

1 tablespoon extra-virgin olive oil
1 red onion, diced
2 cloves fresh garlic, minced
Sea salt
2 teaspoons grated fresh ginger, juice extracted
1 tablespoon mirin
4 cups diced carrots
1 cup peeled and diced butternut squash
5 cups spring or filtered water
½ cup shelled hempseed
1 to 2 scallions, thinly sliced on the diagonal

Place the oil in a soup pot. Add the onion and garlic and place over medium heat. When the onion begins to sizzle, add a pinch of salt and sauté for 1 to 2 minutes. Stir in the ginger juice and mirin and sauté for 1 minute. Stir in the carrots and squash and sauté until shiny with oil. Add the water, cover, and bring to a boil. Reduce the heat to low and cook until the carrots are quite soft, about 40 minutes. Season to taste with salt and simmer 5 minutes longer. Transfer the soup to a food processor or food mill and purée until smooth. Return to the soup pot and simmer 2 to 3 minutes. To serve, spoon the soup into individual bowls and sprinkle with the hempseed and scallions.

In cooler weather, or whenever we need a bit of extra strength, sweet root vegetable soups are just the ticket. Add a bit of ginger to stimulate the circulation and hempseed for essential fatty acids and you've got rocket fuel in a cup.

Wild Thing Soup

Makes 6 to 7 servings

2 teaspoons extra-virgin olive oil

2 teaspoons curry powder

1 yellow onion, minced

1 clove fresh garlic, minced

Sea salt

1 cup diced Yukon gold potatoes

2 teaspoons mirin

4 to 5 cups spring or filtered water

2 teaspoons sweet white miso

4 cups mixed wild, bitter greens (such as dandelion, watercress, arugula, and nettle), well rinsed and finely chopped

½ cup shelled hempseed

1 red bell pepper, roasted over an open flame, peeled, seeded, and diced (see page 63)

Combine the oil and curry powder in a soup pot. Place over medium heat and sauté for 1 minute. Stir in the onion and garlic along with a pinch of salt and sauté for 1 to 2 minutes. Do not brown the onion. Stir in the potatoes and mirin and sauté for 2 minutes. Add the water, cover, and bring to a boil. Reduce the heat to low and cook until the potatoes are soft, about 30 minutes. Remove a few tablespoons of the broth and combine it with the miso. Stir this mixture into soup. Stir in the greens and simmer for 3 to 4 minutes. To serve, spoon the soup into individual bowls and sprinkle with the hempseed and roasted bell pepper.

Come spring, we need to revitalize our bodies so that we feel as light and renewed as the crocus plants sprouting up around us. This refreshing soup is as delicious as it is nourishing. It includes bitter greens to lighten our spirits and hempseed to keep us deeply satisfied.

salads

Salads are much more than wilted lettu
with a few pale tomatoes and cucumbers smothered in bottled
Thousand Island dressing. Great salads are uplifting—their light,
crisp energy refreshes our bodies and our spirits.

No matter what the ingredients, salads add
vitality that is invaluable to us. They relax our middle organs,
stimulate digestion, release stagnant energy from deep within
our bodies, and cool us when the weather is hot or our food is
heavy. Salads are brilliant in their ability to balance our energy,
adding just the right touch of freshness when we need it.

Grains, beans, and vegetables, properly
cooked and combined, come together to create salads that are
limited only by our imaginations. For increased essential fatty
acids, add hempseed oil and shelled hempseed to any dressing.

—Christina

dressings

What's a salad without dressing?
While my personal favorite is a simple dressing of avocado and
hempseed oils, fresh lemon juice, and sea salt, here are some unique
options for creating the salad of your dreams. They are delicious
and high in essential fatty acids.

—Christina

Arugula Salad with Scallion
Vinaigrette and Red Grapes

Makes 4 to 6 servings

Arugula Salad:

1 bunch arugula, rinsed well, tips trimmed

2 to 3 cups seedless red grapes

2 ripe tomatoes, diced

1 cucumber, peeled and diced

4 to 5 red radishes, diced

2 to 3 fresh scallions, thinly sliced on the diagonal

Scallion Vinaigrette:

½ cup shelled hempseed

2 to 3 fresh scallions, thinly sliced

⅓ cup extra-virgin olive oil

3 tablespoons red wine vinegar

2 tablespoons balsamic vinegar

Sea salt

Here is a brilliant summer salad, filled with the abundance of the season. Bitter arugula and fresh tomatoes join forces to keep our energy light and aid the body in releasing internal heat, so we can stay cool as the cucumbers we enjoy all season long.

Clean the arugula and arrange it on a platter. Chill thoroughly.

Combine the grapes, tomatoes, cucumber, radishes, and scallions in a large bowl. Set aside while making the dressing.

Heat a dry skillet over low heat. Stir in the hempseed and lightly toast it until fragrant, about 3 minutes. Transfer the hempseed to a suribachi (grinding bowl) and grind it until half broken. Add the scallions and grind to a paste. Transfer to a small bowl and add the oil, vinegars, and a light seasoning of salt. Whisk until well blended. Adjust the seasonings to your taste. Fold the dressing into the vegetables and toss gently until evenly coated. To serve, mound the vegetables onto the bed of chilled arugula.

HempNut Cookbook

Winter Salad with Hempseed Vinaigrette

Makes 6 to 8 servings

Winter Salad:

2 fennel bulbs

1 large head romaine lettuce, rinsed well and hand-shredded

2 heads frisée (curly endive), rinsed well and hand-shredded

4 to 5 Belgian endives, halved lengthwise and thinly sliced lengthwise

1 small bunch flat-leaf parsley, minced

5 to 6 red radishes, thinly sliced

Hempseed Vinaigrette:

⅓ cup shelled hempseed

¾ cup extra-virgin olive oil

2 to 3 shallots, minced

¼ cup brown rice vinegar

2 tablespoons stoneground mustard

Sea salt

Anise-scented fennel joins forces with nutty hempseed to create a powerfully delicious winter salad. But that's not the best part. Sure, the vegetables are jam-packed with nutrients, fiber, vitamins, and minerals; but by adding hempseed, you get the added punch of essential fatty acids, omega-3 and omega-6.

Trim the fennel stalks flush with the bulbs and discard the stalks, reserving about 3 tablespoons of the leaves. Cut the fennel bulbs in half, remove the cores, and slice each half very thinly. Combine with the romaine, frisée, Belgian endives, parsley, and radishes in a large bowl and set aside.

To make the vinaigrette, heat a dry skillet over low heat and pan toast the hempseed for 2 to 3 minutes or until fragrant. Transfer to a small bowl and set aside. Place the oil and shallots in a small saucepan and warm for 4 to 5 minutes over low heat. Remove from the heat and whisk in the vinegar, mustard, and salt to taste until smooth. Whisk in the toasted hempseed until well combined. Spoon over the vegetables and toss to coat. Serve immediately.

Carrot Salad

Makes 4 to 5 servings

6 carrots, cut into fine matchsticks
2 tablespoons shelled hempseed
6 tablespoons hempseed oil
Grated zest of 1 lemon (2 to 3 teaspoons)
2 cloves fresh garlic, thinly sliced
Sea salt
2 tablespoons fresh lemon juice
5 or 6 oil-cured black olives, pitted and minced
2 or 3 sprigs fresh parsley, minced
1 tablespoon balsamic vinegar
2 to 3 cups spring mix, baby greens, or arugula

Bring a small pot of water to a boil and blanch the carrots for 30 seconds. Drain and transfer to a large bowl. Fold in the hempseed.

Place the hempseed oil, lemon zest, garlic, and a generous pinch of salt in a small saucepan and simmer for 3 to 5 minutes over low heat to infuse the oil. Strain and pour over the carrots. Fold in the lemon juice, olives, parsley, and balsamic vinegar and mix well to evenly incorporate. Set aside for 30 minutes before serving so the flavors can develop. Serve on a bed of the greens.

Fresh and delicious, this delicately sweet salad has just a touch of sour to make the natural character of carrots sparkle.

Green Bean Salad

Makes 4 to 5 servings

2 cups whole green beans, tips trimmed, left whole
1 carrot, grated
2 tablespoons shelled hempseed
3 tablespoons hempseed oil
3 shallots, sliced into thin half moons
3 cloves fresh garlic, thinly sliced
Sea salt
3 tablespoons slivered almonds, lightly pan toasted
3 tablespoons fresh lemon juice

Bring a small pot of water to a boil and boil the green beans 2 to 3 minutes or until just crisp-tender. Transfer to a large bowl and gently mix in the grated carrot and hempseed.

Place the hempseed oil in a small skillet over medium heat. Add the shallots, garlic, and a light sprinkle of salt and sauté 2 to 3 minutes or until the shallots are translucent. Remove from the heat and stir in the almonds and lemon juice. To serve, arrange the green beans on a platter and spoon the shallots and almond mixture over the top.

This salad is fresh and crisp with just a touch of rich taste. It makes a light summer side dish that showcases fresh green beans at the peak of their sunny flavor.

Tuscan Slaw

Dressing:

⅓ cup hempseed oil
⅓ cup pitted and minced oil-cured black olives
3 tablespoons balsamic vinegar
Juice of 1 fresh lemon (about 3 tablespoons)
2 to 3 cloves fresh garlic, minced
Generous pinch of crushed red pepper flakes
Sea salt

Slaw:

½ head green cabbage, finely shredded
1 bunch dark leafy greens, stems trimmed, left whole
½ head red cabbage, finely shredded
½ fennel bulb, finely shredded
1 cucumber, thinly sliced on the diagonal
4 to 5 red radishes, thinly sliced
2 heads Belgian endive, finely shredded

Crisp, lightly cooked vegetable dishes are the hallmark of Italian cuisine. In this salad, sweet cabbage joins with bitter greens and aromatic fennel to create the perfect backdrop for the slightly spicy, sweet and sour dressing.

Prepare the dressing before assembling the salad. Combine all the ingredients (use salt to taste, but keep it light) in a small saucepan and place over very low heat. Cook for 7 to 10 minutes, stirring occasionally. This will infuse the flavors into the oil.

While the dressing simmers, bring a pot of water to a boil and cook the green cabbage 2 to 3 minutes or until just limp. Remove the cabbage with a slotted spoon and drain well. In the same water, cook the greens until just wilted, about 2 minutes. Transfer to a cutting board and cut into bite-size pieces. Mix with the cabbage. Finally, in the same water, cook the red cabbage until just limp, about 3 minutes. Drain and add to the cabbage and greens. Mix in the fennel, cucumber, and radishes and toss to combine. Just before serving, toss the slaw with the raw endive and hot dressing. Serve immediately.

Thai Cabbage Salad

3 cups finely diced red cabbage
2 cups finely diced green cabbage
2 cups bite-size cauliflower florets
1 avocado, finely diced
½ cup shelled hempseed
½ cup minced fresh cilantro
¼ cup extra virgin olive oil
¼ cup brown rice syrup
¼ cup soy sauce
3 tablespoons umeboshi vinegar
1 tablespoon grated orange zest
1 inch fresh ginger, juice extracted
1 clove fresh garlic, minced
Generous pinch of chili powder

Combine all the ingredients in a large bowl and toss gently. Set aside to marinate for at least 30 minutes before serving.

Note: You can make this dish more digestible by lightly blanching the cabbage and cauliflower.

Enjoy the exotic flavors of Thailand with this unusual salad. It incorporates enzymes from a wide variety of fresh vegetables and protein and essential fatty acids from hempseed.

Tabouli Salad

Makes 3 to 4 servings

2 cups spring or filtered water
1¼ cups bulgur (cracked wheat)
1 ripe tomato, diced
1 small cucumber, diced
1 bunch fresh parsley, minced
¼ cup chopped fresh mint
¼ cup shelled hempseed
⅓ cup pitted and coarsely chopped oil-cured black olives
2 or 3 scallions, minced
Juice of 1 fresh lemon (about 3 tablespoons)
3 tablespoons extra-virgin olive oil
2 tablespoons hempseed oil
Sea salt

Bring the water to a boil and stir in the bulgur. Cover and remove from the heat. Allow to stand undisturbed for 15 to 20 minutes or until all the liquid has been absorbed into the grain. Fluff the bulgur with a fork and transfer to a large bowl. Stir in the remaining ingredients, adding salt to taste. Cover and chill thoroughly before serving.

Tabouli is a Middle Eastern tradition. This grain salad is the perfect warm-weather side dish, laced with fresh vegetables and fragrant with mint.

Kale HempNut Salad

1 bunch of kale, finely chopped
1 ripe tomato, diced
½ cup shelled hempseed
2 tablespoons extra-virgin olive oil or hempseed oil
2 tablespoons fresh lemon juice
¾ teaspoon sea salt
½ teaspoon chili powder

Combine all the ingredients in a large bowl and toss gently. Let marinate for at least 30 minutes before serving.

This salad is so easy and tasty. Until this recipe, I never knew kale could be so delicious fresh and uncooked. If you want to make it easier to digest, lightly steam the kale before making the salad.

Hemp Mayo

Makes about 1 cup

4 ounces soft tofu, boiled for 5 minutes
¼ cup extra-virgin olive oil
3 tablespoons fresh lemon juice
2 tablespoons shelled hempseed, ground into a fine meal
2 teaspoons brown rice syrup
Sea salt

Place all the ingredients except the salt in a food processor and purée until smooth and thick. Season with salt to taste and purée again to incorporate.

Need a creamy, rich, vegan mayo for sandwiches and salads? Look no further.

Sweetie-Pie Dressing

Makes about 2 cups

1 cup brown rice syrup
⅓ cup extra-virgin olive oil
⅓ cup hempseed oil
3 tablespoons stoneground mustard
3 tablespoons shelled hempseed
3 tablespoons red wine vinegar
2 to 3 shallots, minced
Generous pinch of sea salt

Whisk all ingredients briskly to emulsify the oil and thoroughly combine. Adjust the seasoning to suit your taste.

They say that the sweet ain't as sweet without the bitter. Well, in this dressing, sweet is the star of the show, with just enough bitter to make it all the sweeter. And with nutrient-dense hempseed and oil—how sweet it is!

Quick French Dressing

Makes about 1 cup

⅓ cup extra-virgin olive oil
⅓ cup hempseed oil
3 tablespoons red wine vinegar
3 tablespoons brown rice syrup
2 tablespoons shelled hempseed, ground into a fine meal
1 teaspoon onion powder
1 teaspoon paprika
1 teaspoon sea salt

Place all the ingredients in a small bowl and whisk briskly until the oils emulsify. Transfer to a glass jar and shake well before using.

Note: Stored in the refrigerator, this dressing will keep for about ten days.

You can buy bottled French dressing and hope for the best for your fresh salad, or you can make this simple, delicious version and treat your salad and your palate to the very finest.

Sweet and Sour Lemon Dressing

Makes 1 cup

8 ounces soft tofu, boiled for 5 minutes, drained well
¼ cup brown rice syrup
3 tablespoons sweet white miso
Juice of 1 fresh lemon (about 3 tablespoons)
2 tablespoons shelled hempseed, ground into a fine meal
2 tablespoons sesame tahini
1 tablespoon umeboshi vinegar
2 to 3 sprigs fresh parsley, minced
Grated zest of 1 fresh lemon (2 to 3 teaspoons)
Spring or filtered water

Place all the ingredients except the water in a food processor and purée until smooth. Slowly add enough water to create the consistency you desire. Adjust the seasonings to suit your taste.

This dressing adds just the right touch to lightly cooked vegetables and fresh salads. The mild sour taste, with a hint of sweet, will take your veggies from boring to bold. When you see how easy it is to make, you'll think you've gone to heaven.

side dishes

Side dishes are those little additions that turn the main attraction into a meal. Silky whole grains serve as the backdrop for any feast. Beans are sensual and deeply nourishing, providing us with protein and a gentle source of strength. And then there are the vegetable dishes and fresh, crisp salads that dance on our tongues. We can create quick sautéed dishes, rich with oil, lightly cooked to make us feel vital and strong. Cooking long, sensual, stewed vegetables will make us feel warm and cozy, relaxed and calm. Quick or crisp, stewed or roasted, side dishes help draw the line between a snack and an unforgettable meal.

—Christina

Baked Onion Slices

Makes 4 to 8 servings

2 large red onions, sliced into 2-inch-thick rings
Extra-virgin olive oil
Sea salt
Mirin
Finely grated zest of 1 fresh lemon (2 to 3 teaspoons)
4 to 5 sprigs fresh parsley, minced
½ cup shelled hempseed

Preheat the oven to 350°F. Arrange the onion slices in a single layer on a dry baking sheet. Sprinkle generously with olive oil and sprinkle lightly with salt and mirin. Cover tightly with foil and bake for 40 minutes. Uncover and return to the oven for 7 to 10 minutes or until the onions start to brown.

While the onions bake, prepare the topping. Combine the lemon zest and parsley and mix well. Lightly pan toast the hempseed in a dry skillet over low heat. Stir into the lemon zest and parsley and mix well. Season lightly with salt and stir until well combined.

When the onions are ready, remove from the oven and transfer to a serving platter. Mound some of the topping on each onion slice and serve.

Rich, sweet, and packed with nutrition, especially hard-to-get essential fatty acids, this dish not only takes its place as one of the great side dishes for any dinner or buffet table, but you get the additional pleasure of feeding your loved ones the finest food in its most delicious form.

Roasted Sweet Potatoes with
Apricots and Curried Hempseed

Makes 4 to 6 servings

3 to 4 garnet or jewel sweet potatoes, cut into large chunks
6 to 8 dried apricots, cut in half
Extra-virgin olive oil
Grated zest of 2 fresh lemons (4 to 6 teaspoons)
Sea salt
1 teaspoon curry powder
½ cup shelled hempseed
2 to 3 sprigs fresh parsley, minced

Preheat the oven to 375°F. Arrange the sweet potatoes and apricots in a single layer in a large baking dish. Drizzle generously with olive oil, and sprinkle with the lemon zest and salt. Cover tightly and bake for 45 minutes. Uncover and return to the oven for 7 to 10 minutes or until the sweet potatoes are lightly browned.

While the potatoes roast, place the curry powder in a dry skillet over medium heat. Dry roast the curry powder for 1 to 2 minutes. Reduce the heat to low and stir in the hempseed. Toast, stirring constantly, until the curry powder turns from orange to a vivid yellow; it will return to a lovely orange color as it cools. To serve, sprinkle the cooked sweet potatoes with the curried hempseed and fresh parsley.

Note: The curried hempseed condiment may be made in advance. Transfer it to a glass jar and let it cool completely before sealing. It will keep for 1 to 2 weeks stored at room temperature.

This luscious, sweet side dish is the epitome of autumn—warming to the body, satisfying, rich, and good for us.

HempNut Cookbook

String Beans à la HempNut

Makes 3 to 4 servings

4 cups fresh string beans, tips trimmed, cut into 2-inch pieces
Extra-virgin olive oil
1 small red onion, sliced into thin half-moons
1 to 2 cloves fresh garlic, thinly sliced
Sea salt
2 teaspoons mirin
¼ cup shelled hempseed
Juice of 1 fresh lemon (about 3 tablespoons)

Steam the green beans until bright green and crisp-tender, about 3 minutes. Drain and set aside to cool.

Place a small amount of olive oil in a skillet. Add the onion and garlic and place over medium heat. When the onion begins to sizzle, add a pinch of salt and sauté until the onion is limp, about 2 minutes. Season with salt to taste and add the mirin. Reduce the heat to low and cook, uncovered, until any liquid has evaporated. Remove from the heat and stir in the hempseed and lemon juice. To serve, arrange the steamed green beans on a platter and spoon the onion mixture over them. Serve immediately.

Crisp and bright green, with the satisfying, nutty taste of hempseed, this side dish is sure to win raves.

Asparagus with Crunchy HempNut

Makes 3 to 4 servings

1 to 2 pounds fresh asparagus
1 tablespoon extra-virgin olive oil
1 tablespoon spring or filtered water
1 tablespoon balsamic vinegar
Sea salt
¼ cup shelled hempseed
Generous pinch of curry powder
1 to 2 sprigs fresh parsley, minced

Snap off the tough end of the asparagus stems. (Snapping them rather than cutting them ensures that the asparagus will not take on a bitter flavor.) Place the oil, water, vinegar, and a generous pinch of salt in a deep skillet. Arrange the asparagus in the oil mixture, cover, and turn the heat to medium. When you hear a light sizzle in the pan, reduce the heat to low and cook until the asparagus is bright green and tender.

While the asparagus cooks, heat a small dry skillet. Add the hempseed and curry powder and pan toast them over low heat until just fragrant, about 2 minutes.

To serve, arrange the asparagus on a platter and sprinkle with the crunchy, seasoned hempseed and the parsley.

Spring means asparagus. Asparagus means fresh. Add the magic of hempseed and the richness of avocado oil and you have the perfect warm-weather side dish.

Winter Squash with HempNut Filling

Makes 6 to 8 servings

Extra-virgin olive oil

1 small yellow onion, diced

1 to 2 cloves fresh garlic, minced

Sea salt

1 Granny Smith apple, peeled, cored, and diced

1 stalk celery, diced

Grated zest of 1 fresh lemon (2 to 3 teaspoons)

¼ cup golden raisins

⅓ cup shelled hempseed

1 tablespoon hempseed oil

2 to 3 sprigs fresh parsley, minced

2 winter squash, halved and seeded (good choices are acorn, butternut, or hokkaido pumpkin)

Preheat the oven to 350°F. Place a small amount of olive oil in a skillet. Add the onion and garlic and place over medium heat. When the onion begins to sizzle, add a pinch of salt and sauté for 1 to 2 minutes. Stir in the apple, celery, and lemon zest, and season lightly with salt . Sauté for 2 to 3 minutes. Remove from the heat and stir in the raisins, hempseed, hempseed oil, and parsley.

Arrange the squash in a baking dish, and spoon the filling mixture evenly into the cavities of the squash. Pour ½ inch of water in the dish. Cover tightly with foil and bake for 40 minutes. Uncover and bake until the squash is quite tender and the filling is lightly browned, about 15 minutes longer. To serve, slice the stuffed squash halves into 3 or 4 wedges.

Enjoy this scrumptious, sweet winter squash, baked to perfection and deliciously balanced with the rich, nutty flavor of hempseed. I can't think of a more wonderful, special occasion side dish.

Mixed Vegetable Stir-Fry

Makes 4 to 5 servings

2 tablespoons extra-virgin olive oil

1 small leek, well rinsed and thinly sliced on the diagonal

½-inch piece fresh ginger, cut into thin matchsticks

2 cloves fresh garlic, thinly sliced

Natural soy sauce

1 carrot, cut into thin matchsticks

1 cup thinly sliced daikon, cut into thin matchsticks

1 small zucchini, cut into thin matchsticks

1 to 2 stalks broccoli, broken into very small florets

2 tablespoons mirin

Grated zest of 1 fresh orange (about 1½ tablespoons)

⅓ cup shelled hempseed

1 to 2 scallions, thinly sliced on the diagonal

Brown rice vinegar

Place the olive oil in a wok and place over medium heat. Add the leek, ginger, garlic, and a splash of soy sauce and stir-fry until the leek is bright green; this will take under 1 minute. Stir in the carrot and daikon, add another splash of soy sauce, and stir-fry for 2 minutes. Stir in the zucchini and broccoli, season lightly with soy sauce, and stir-fry for 1 to 2 minutes. Add the mirin and orange zest and stir-fry until the vegetables are just crisp-tender. Remove from the heat and transfer to a serving platter. Sprinkle lightly with the hempseed, scallions, and rice vinegar to taste. Serve immediately.

Once you've tasted this light, crisp, refreshing dish, you'll have no more excuses for living on drive-thru food!

Stuffed Artichokes

Makes 2 servings

¼ cup shelled hempseed
¼ cup pine nuts, finely chopped
Extra-virgin olive oil
2 to 3 sprigs fresh parsley, minced
2 cloves fresh garlic, minced
Sea salt
2 medium globe artichokes
1 cup dry white wine
1 fresh lemon

To prepare the stuffing, combine the hempseed, pine nuts, 2 to 3 tablespoons of olive oil, parsley, garlic, and salt to taste in a small bowl. Using a fork, mix the ingredients to make a coarse meal.

To prepare the artichokes, trim the sharp tips off each leaf with scissors. With a sharp knife, slice the stems flush with the bottom of the artichokes (reserve the stems). Then slice off the top quarter of each artichoke. Stand the artichoke on its bottom and gently press to spread open the leaves. Using a grapefruit spoon, scoop the choke out of the center. Spoon half of the stuffing into the center of the each artichoke. Arrange the stuffed artichokes in a deep saucepan. Peel the stems and place them on top of each artichoke. Pour the wine in the pan, drizzle lightly with olive oil, and sprinkle lightly with salt. Slice the lemon in half and place it in the saucepan next to the artichokes. Cover and bring to a boil over medium heat. Reduce the heat to low, cover, and cook 30 to 35 minutes or until the artichokes are tender.

Artichokes are one of the greatest joys of nature. Delicious, sensual, and slightly exotic, artichokes are one of my favorite vegetables. Try this richly flavored stuffed version just once and you'll agree.

Baba Ganouj

Makes about 2 cups

2 medium eggplants
½ cup chopped fresh parsley
Juice of 2 fresh lemons (about 6 tablespoons)
¼ cup shelled hempseed
1 tablespoon hempseed oil
3 cloves fresh garlic, thinly sliced
1 teaspoon sea salt
Pepper

Preheat the oven to 400°F. Prick each eggplant five or six times with a fork. Place directly on the center oven rack and bake 45 to 60 minutes or until the skins pierce easily with a fork. Remove from the oven and cool enough to handle. Slice lengthwise and scoop out the flesh. Transfer the flesh to a food processor along with the parsley, lemon juice, hempseed, hempseed oil, garlic, salt, and pepper to taste. Purée until smooth. Adjust the seasonings to suit your taste and purée again. Serve at room temperature or chilled, with crackers, chips, or sliced raw vegetables.

This traditional Middle Eastern favorite gets an extra burst of nutrition and nutty flavor from lightly toasted, shelled hempseed. Creamy, delicious, and jam-packed with essential fatty acids—it's a real winner.

Broiled Tomatoes with Garlic

Makes 2 servings

2 tablespoons extra-virgin olive oil

Grated zest of 1 fresh lemon (2 to 3 teaspoons)

1 teaspoon chopped fresh parsley

1 clove fresh garlic, minced

Sea salt

2 ripe tomatoes, stemmed and cut in half

2 tablespoons shelled hempseed

Preheat the broiler. Combine the olive oil, lemon zest, parsley, garlic, and salt to taste with a fork to create a coarse paste. Spread evenly over the cut sides of the tomato halves. Sprinkle with the hempseed. Broil for 3 to 5 minutes or until the edges of the tomatoes are lightly browned.

Nothing announces summer quite like fresh tomatoes. Did you know that the important lycopene is absorbed four times more efficiently if the tomatoes are lightly cooked? Add the dense nutrients of hempseed and you have the makings for a perfectly nourishing summer dish—light, rich, and satisfying.

Stuffed Mushrooms

Makes 6 to 8 servings

24 medium to large button mushrooms

3 to 4 tablespoons extra-virgin olive oil

3 to 4 cloves fresh garlic, minced

2 to 3 shallots, minced

Grated zest of 1 fresh lemon (2 to 3 teaspoons)

2 to 3 sprigs fresh parsley, minced

1 teaspoon sweet white miso, dissolved in
    2 tablespoons warm water

1 teaspoon mirin

Generous pinch of dried rosemary

Generous pinch of dried thyme

¼ cup shelled hempseed

¼ cup whole wheat bread crumbs

Sea salt

Olive oil

An earthy, richly flavored starter dish, stuffed mushrooms are lovely on a buffet table. Try them served on a pool of Carrot Coulis, page 109, or as a side dish for an elegant dinner. They require a bit of effort, but it will be worth every second.

Preheat the oven to 375°F. Wipe the mushrooms with a clean, damp paper towel and remove the stems. Coarsely chop the stems and set aside. Rub each mushroom lightly with olive oil and place them stem-side up on a baking sheet. Bake for 2 to 3 minutes. Remove from the oven and set aside to cool.

Place the remaining olive oil in a skillet. Add the garlic and shallots and place over medium heat. When the shallots begin to sizzle, stir in the lemon zest, parsley, miso, mirin, rosemary, and thyme and sauté for 2 to 3 minutes. Remove from the heat and stir in the hempseed and bread crumbs. Adjust the salt to your taste. Fill the mushroom caps abundantly, packing the filling. Bake 10 to 12 minutes or until the mushrooms are tender and the filling is lightly browned. Transfer to a serving platter and drizzle lightly with a fruity olive oil. Serve immediately.

Spicy Soba Noodles

Makes about 4 servings

1 (8-ounce) package soba noodles

1 to 2 tablespoons light sesame oil

1 small leek, well rinsed and thinly sliced on the diagonal

2 to 3 cloves fresh garlic, minced

3 to 4 thin slices fresh ginger, cut into fine matchsticks

1 teaspoon chili powder

Natural soy sauce

1 red bell pepper, roasted over an open flame, peeled, seeded,
    and sliced into thin ribbons (see page 63)

½ cup lightly brewed green tea

3 scallions, thinly sliced on the diagonal

¼ cup shelled hempseed

1 tablespoon brown rice vinegar

2 teaspoons brown rice syrup

Soba noodles are unlike any other noodles. Made from buckwheat, they warm our bodies and make us feel strong and vital. This dish adds hot spices to stimulate our circulation and hempseed for essential fatty acids. These are no ordinary noodles!

Bring a large pot of water to a boil and cook the soba noodles al dente. Drain and rinse well. (Soba noodles are usually tossed with salt in the drying process, and if they are not rinsed well, they can make the final dish salty.) Set aside.

Heat the sesame oil in a deep skillet. Add the leek, garlic, and ginger and sauté 2 to 3 minutes or until the leek is limp. Stir in the chili powder and a light sprinkle of soy sauce and sauté for 1 to 2 minutes longer. Stir in the roasted red pepper, green tea, scallions, hempseed, vinegar, and rice syrup. Cover, reduce the heat to low, and simmer for 2 to 3 minutes. Uncover and cook until the sauce reduces slightly. Remove from the heat and stir in the cooked soba noodles. Transfer to a serving platter and serve immediately.

Note: Do not make the tea too strong or the flavor of the dish will turn bitter.

Spinach Pasta

2 tablespoons extra-virgin olive oil or hempseed oil

1 red onion, thinly sliced

4 cloves fresh garlic, thinly sliced

Sea salt

Generous pinch of crushed red pepper flakes

1 (6-ounce) jar marinated artichoke hearts, drained
    and halved lengthwise

1 red bell pepper, roasted over an open flame, peeled, seeded,
    and sliced into thin ribbons (see page 63)

Dry white wine

8 ounces whole wheat spinach pasta (fettuccine, spaghetti,
    or capellini are best)

1 tablespoon paprika

¼ cup shelled hempseed

This pasta dish makes a simple, elegant, and colorful side dish or a light main course.

Fill a large pot with water and add a splash of olive oil. Bring to a boil.

Meanwhile, place the olive oil in a deep skillet. Add the red onion and garlic and place over medium heat. When the onion begins to sizzle, add a pinch of salt and red pepper flakes and sauté for 2 to 3 minutes. Stir in the artichoke hearts and roasted red pepper, sprinkle lightly with wine, and season to taste with salt. Reduce the heat to low and cook 5 to 6 minutes or until the artichoke hearts are very tender.

When the water boils, add the pasta and cook it al dente. Drain well, reserving about ½ cup of the cooking water. Do not rinse the pasta.

While the pasta cooks, heat a dry skillet over medium heat. Add the paprika and dry roast it for 1 minute. Stir in the hempseed and dry roast it with the paprika until fragrant, about 3 minutes. Set aside.

Stir the reserved pasta cooking water into the sautéed vegetables, stirring until the mixture thickens slightly. Remove from the heat and stir in the cooked pasta. Transfer to a serving platter and sprinkle generously with the toasted hempseed. Serve immediately.

Polenta

Makes 6 to 8 servings

5 cups spring or filtered water
1 cup coarse yellow corn grits
Generous pinch of sea salt
2 tablespoons shelled hempseed
Extra-virgin olive oil

Place the water, corn grits, and salt in a saucepan. Bring to a boil over medium heat, whisking constantly. Reduce the heat to low and cook, whisking frequently to avoid lumping. As the polenta cooks, it will thicken and turn creamy. It's ready when the center of the polenta bubbles and pops, about 25 minutes. When the polenta is ready, whisk in the hempseed and a generous drizzle of olive oil for a buttery flavor and smooth texture. Serve immediately for a soft polenta. For a firm polenta, transfer it to a lightly oiled pie plate and set aside until firm. It can then be sliced and pan fried.

Variation: For a more strongly flavored polenta, add dried basil to taste at the beginning of cooking, or shredded fresh basil at the end of cooking.

This traditional Italian grain dish is usually paired with richly flavored stewed vegetables. The delicate taste of the cornmeal provides the perfect backdrop for any strong flavors. With the addition of hempseed, this polenta isn't quite as mild-mannered anymore—at least nutritionally.

Nori Rolls

Makes 6 to 8 servings

Nori Rolls:

3 to 4 sheets toasted sushi nori
2 cups cooked brown rice, cooled to room temperature
½ cup shelled hempseed
Stoneground mustard
2 carrots, cut lengthwise into long strips, boiled for 1 minute and drained
2 to 3 scallions, greens only, cut into long strips
½ cucumber, split lengthwise and sliced into long strips

Dipping Sauce:

1 cup spring or filtered water
2 to 3 tablespoons natural soy sauce
1 to 2 teaspoons fresh ginger juice
Brown rice vinegar
Toasted sesame oil

To make the nori rolls, lay a sushi mat or kitchen towel on a dry, flat work surface. Lay a sheet of the nori on the mat, shiny side down. Combine the rice and hempseed and mix well. Press the rice firmly onto the nori, about ¼ inch thick, covering the nori completely widthwise, but leaving a ½-inch margin of nori exposed at the edges closest to and furthest from you. Spread a thin ribbon of mustard horizontally along the rice, starting at the edge closest to you. Lay 1 carrot, cucumber, and scallion strip on the mustard. Using the mat as a guide, roll the nori around the rice, jelly-roll style, gently pressing as you roll, to create a tight cylinder. Set aside the nori roll, seam-side down, and repeat with the remaining ingredients.

Nori rolls are light and fresh, but they satisfy us like nothing else. This special version of nori rolls contains whole grains for sustained energy, sea plants for minerals, fresh crisp vegetables to refresh us, and hempseed for all the nutrition a healthy body needs. They make the perfect side dish, snack, or exotic lunch.

To prepare the dipping sauce, combine the water, soy sauce, ginger juice, and vinegar and oil to taste in a small bowl. Whisk until well blended.

Wet a sharp knife and slice each nori roll into 8 equal pieces. Arrange the pieces, cut-side up, on a platter and serve with the dipping sauce on the side.

Carrot Coulis

Makes about 2 cups

2 teaspoons hempseed oil
2 to 3 shallots, minced
Sea salt
5 or 6 medium carrots, diced
Mirin
Spring or filtered water

Place the oil in a deep skillet. Add the shallots and place over medium heat. When the shallots begin to sizzle, add a pinch of salt and sauté for 1 minute. Take care not to brown the shallots. Stir in the carrots and sprinkle lightly with mirin. Add enough water to partially cover the carrots and season lightly with salt. Cover and cook for 7 to 10 minutes or until the carrots are quite soft. Uncover and cook until the remaining liquid has reduced but not disappeared.

Transfer the carrots to a food processor or food mill and purée until completely smooth. Return to the stove top and turn the heat to low. Slowly whisk in enough water to create a thin sauce.

Here is a simple but elegant sauce to pool under any number of savory dishes. Delicately sweet, this smooth sauce is the perfect backdrop for any strongly flavored dish.

main dishes

Ah, the main event, the main course. Most Americans are used to the idea of the main attraction on their plate being meat, fish, or chicken. In natural whole foods cooking, however, everything is the main attraction (lucky us!). It's all so good, it would be difficult to decide who is the star. But in the interest of comfort, here are dishes you can serve as a main course for those occasions when you want to feature one particular specialty.

—Christina

Vegetarian Sausage

Makes 3 cans of vegetarian sausage
(5 to 6 slices per can)

1½ cups whole wheat pastry flour

1½ cups plain soymilk

1 cup shelled hempseed

1 cup nutritional yeast flakes

½ cup soy flour

⅓ cup extra-virgin olive oil

1 tablespoon garlic powder

1 tablespoon natural soy sauce

1 tablespoon barley malt

1 tablespoon prepared mustard

1 teaspoon ground anise or fennel seed

1 teaspoon ground allspice

1 teaspoon dried oregano

1 teaspoon dried sage

1 teaspoon sea salt

½ teaspoon pepper

¼ teaspoon cayenne

Okay, okay, there are a lot of ingredients in this one. But you have a choice. You can either purchase vegetarian sausage that's loaded with compromised ingredients, or you can do a bit of work and make your own wholesome, delicious version.

Combine all the ingredients in a large bowl. Mix well until evenly blended. Oil 3 clean, empty, 16-ounce tin cans. Fill each can flush to the top. Cover with wax paper and then aluminum foil. Secure with a rubber band. Stand the cans, open-side up, in a deep pot. Add water to cover the cans halfway, cover, and bring to a rolling boil. Reduce the heat to low and steam for 1 hour and 15 minutes. Carefully remove the cans from the pot and cool completely. Once cooled, the sausage can be sliced and pan fried or baked.

Chickpea Salad with Tomatoes and Chipotle

Makes 3 to 4 servings

1-inch piece kombu
1½ cups dried chickpeas, sorted and rinsed
5 cups spring or filtered water
⅓ cup sesame tahini
Juice from 1 fresh lime (about 2 tablespoons)
2 teaspoons extra-virgin olive oil
2 teaspoons brown rice syrup
1 teaspoon sea salt
3 to 4 plum tomatoes, diced
½ red onion, finely diced
½ cup minced fresh cilantro
1 tablespoon finely minced canned chipotle
½ teaspoon ground cumin
½ cup shelled hempseed, lightly pan toasted (see note below)

Summertime calls for light, fresh food with a bit of spice to keep us cool. But we still need substance to feel satisfied. This bean salad fits the bill perfectly, with chickpeas, a creamy dressing, fresh juicy summer tomatoes, and just a touch of heat and smoky flavor from chipotle.

Place the kombu on the bottom of a pressure cooker, with the beans and water on top. Bring to a boil, uncovered. Seal the lid and bring to full pressure. Reduce the heat to low and cook for 40 minutes. Allow the pressure to reduce naturally, open the lid, and check the beans for tenderness. If they are too hard, continue cooking until tender. If they are done to your satisfaction, drain and transfer to a large bowl.

For the dressing, combine the tahini, lime juice, olive oil, rice syrup and salt in a small bowl and whisk until smooth.

Add the tomatoes, onion, cilantro, chipotle, and cumin to the cooked beans and stir in the dressing to coat. Transfer to a serving bowl and garnish with the hempseed.

Note: To pan toast hempseed, simply place a dry skillet over medium heat. When the skillet is hot, add the hempseed. Cook and stir until slightly puffed and fragrant, about 2 to 3 minutes.

Hemp 'n' Rice Croquettes

Makes 4 to 6 servings

Extra-virgin olive oil

1 yellow onion, diced

1 teaspoon dried thyme

Sea salt

2 cups cooked sweet brown rice

1 cup shelled hempseed

½ cup coarse whole wheat bread crumbs

¼ cup rolled oats

Yellow cornmeal

3 cups spring or filtered water

1 yellow onion, sliced into thin half moons

4 teaspoons barley miso

2 to 3 scallions, thinly sliced on the diagonal

Lightly fried and served in a pool of savory broth, these rich, flavorful, nutrient-packed croquettes make a delicious side dish, starter, or light lunch.

Place a small amount of olive oil in a skillet. Add the diced onion and place over medium heat. When the onion begins to sizzle, add the thyme and a pinch of salt and sauté for 2 to 3 minutes.

Combine the cooked rice, hempseed, bread crumbs, and rolled oats in a large bowl. Stir in the sautéed onion. The mixture should hold together well and will be a bit stiff. Form into 2-inch discs. Dredge each croquette in cornmeal.

Place about ½ inch of olive oil in a deep skillet and place over medium heat. When the oil is hot (patterns will form in the oil, known as "dancing"), fry the croquettes until crisp and golden, turning once to ensure even browning. Drain on paper towels and place on a baking sheet in a warm oven while preparing the remainder of the croquettes.

While the croquettes are frying, place the water and sliced onion in a saucepan and bring to a boil. Cover and reduce the heat to low. Cook until the onions are soft, about 6 minutes. Remove a small amount of the cooking broth and dissolve the miso in it. Stir the thinned miso back into the onions and simmer 3 to 4 minutes longer. Serve the croquettes in a bowl with the onions and broth. Garnish with the scallions.

Vegetarian Holiday Roast

Makes 8 to 10 servings

1½ cups green or brown lentils, sorted and rinsed well

1½ cups sweet brown rice, rinsed well

1 cup yellow millet, rinsed well

9 cups spring or filtered water

1 or 2 bay leaves

Sea salt

½ cup shelled hempseed

3 slices whole grain sourdough bread, coarsely crumbled

½ cup almond butter

3 tablespoons extra-virgin olive oil or hempseed oil

1 cup finely diced onions

3 cloves fresh garlic, minced

1 cup finely diced butternut squash

1 or 2 stalks celery, diced

1 cup mirin or dry white wine

2 heaping teaspoons chopped dried sage

1 teaspoon dried rosemary

½ teaspoon celery seeds

½ bunch parsley, rinsed and left whole

Preheat the oven to 350°F and lightly oil a large loaf pan.

Place the lentils, brown rice, and millet in a pressure cooker. Add the water and bring to a boil over high heat. Allow the mixture to boil uncovered for 5 minutes. Add the bay leaves and a generous pinch of salt. Seal the lid and bring to full pressure. Reduce the heat to low and cook for 45 minutes. Remove the from the heat and allow the pressure to reduce naturally. Open the lid (the mixture should be quite soft) and stir gently to combine.

While the lentils and grains cook, combine the hempseed, crumbled bread, and almond butter in a large bowl and set aside.

Place a small amount of olive oil in a skillet. Add the onions and garlic and turn the heat to medium. When the onions begin to sizzle, add a pinch of salt and sauté for 2 to 3 minutes, just until the onions begin to color. Stir in the squash and celery and season to taste with salt. Add about 1 cup of mirin and the sage, rosemary, and celery seeds. Cook uncovered over low heat, stirring frequently, until the vegetables are tender and the wine has thickened slightly, about 8 minutes.

To make the roast, stir the cooked lentils and grains and the sautéed mixture into the bread and hempseed. Mix well to combine. Press into the prepared pan and cover with foil. Bake for 35 minutes. Remove the cover and bake for another 25 to 30 minutes or until the top has browned and the loaf is firm to the touch. Remove from the oven and allow to cool for 20 minutes before slicing.

To serve, arrange the parsley sprigs on a platter. Cut the roast into slices and arrange over the parsley. Serve with Caramelized Onion Gravy, page 70.

Here is an excellent main dish that is high in flavor, protein, and fiber, yet low in fat. It's takes a bit of effort to prepare, but it is worth it. Trust me, no one will miss the meat!

Quinoa Pilaf

2 cups spring or filtered water
1 cup quinoa, rinsed well
Sea salt
1 tablespoon extra-virgin olive oil
1 red onion, diced
2 cloves fresh garlic, thinly sliced
½ cup fresh or frozen corn kernels
¼ cup chopped fresh basil or cilantro
1 or 2 stalks celery, diced
¼ cup shelled hempseed
¼ cup coarsely chopped pecans
2 teaspoons hempseed oil

Place the water and quinoa in a saucepan and bring to a boil. Add a pinch of salt, cover and reduce the heat to low. Cook until the quinoa has absorbed all the water and opened, about 30 minutes.

While the quinoa cooks, place the olive oil in a skillet. Add the onion and garlic and place over medium heat. When the onion begins to sizzle, add a pinch of salt and sauté for 2 to 3 minutes. Stir in the corn and basil, season to taste with salt, and sauté for 2 minutes.

When the quinoa is cooked, stir in the sautéed vegetables along with the celery, hempseed, pecans, and hempseed oil. Transfer to a serving bowl and serve warm or chilled.

Quinoa is not only one of the most delicious whole grains, it's also one of the highest in protein and lysine. Combine it with hempseed and you have one power-packed pilaf.

HempNutty Burgers

Makes 6 to 8 burgers

2 cups cooked or canned black beans
1 cup cooked short grain brown rice
½ cup whole wheat bread crumbs
½ cup shelled hempseed
¼ cup rolled oats
2 tablespoons almond butter
Extra-virgin olive oil
1 small onion, diced
1 teaspoon poultry seasoning (equal parts dried parsley, sage,
    rosemary, and thyme)
1 teaspoon sea salt
Generous pinch of chili powder

Combine the black beans, rice, bread crumbs, hempseed, oats, and almond butter in a large bowl.

Place 2 teaspoons of olive oil in a skillet. Add the onion and heat over medium heat. When the onion begins to sizzle, stir in the poultry seasoning, salt, and chili powder and sauté for 2 to 3 minutes. Stir into the bean mixture and mix well. With moist hands, form the mixture into burger-sized patties.

Heat a generous amount of olive oil in a skillet. Pan fry the burgers until golden and crisp on the outside, turning once to ensure even browning on both sides.

Yummy for lunch or a hearty snack, these burgers are rich in protein and essential fatty acids and are surprisingly meaty in a veggie sort of way.

Roots, Rock, Reggae

Makes 6 to 8 servings

3 or 4 Yukon gold potatoes, quartered

2 red onions, halved, each half sliced into 4 wedges

1 or 2 small sweet potatoes, cut into 1-inch irregular chunks

1 small rutabaga, peeled and cut into 1-inch irregular chunks

1 or 2 small golden beets, peeled and cut into 1-inch irregular chunks

1 or 2 carrots, cut into 1-inch irregular chunks

8 ounces tempeh, cut into ½-inch cubes, pan fried until golden
    (see note next page)

3 tablespoons extra-virgin olive oil

2 tablespoons dry white wine

2 tablespoons natural soy sauce

Juice of 2 fresh oranges (⅔ to 1 cup)

Grated zest of 1 fresh orange (about 1½ tablespoons)

½ cup unsweetened shredded coconut

1 tablespoon grated fresh ginger, juice extracted

2 cloves fresh garlic, minced

1 teaspoon curry powder

½ cup shelled hempseed

Sweet, strengthening, and as scrumptious as it gets—I think that accurately describes oven-roasted root vegetables, don't you? A touch of tropical flavors will bring out the reggae in all of us.

Preheat the oven to 400°F. Combine the Yukon gold potatoes, onions, sweet potatoes, rutabaga, beets, carrots, and tempeh in a large bowl. Sprinkle with the oil, wine, and soy sauce, and stir in the orange juice, orange zest, coconut, ginger juice, and garlic. Spread the mixture on a large baking sheet with sides and cover tightly with foil. Bake for 45 minutes. Uncover and return to the oven to lightly brown the vegetables.

While the vegetables bake, heat a dry skillet over medium heat and pan toast the curry powder for 2 to 3 minutes. Stir in the hempseed and pan toast, stirring constantly, until the seeds are fragrant, about 3 minutes.

When the vegetables are finished cooking, remove them from the oven and sprinkle lightly with the curried hempseed.

Note: To pan fry the tempeh, place a generous amount of olive oil or avocado oil in a skillet over medium heat. When the oil is hot, fry the tempeh until golden on both sides, turning once to ensure even browning.

HempNut Rice

Makes 4 servings

1 tablespoon extra-virgin olive oil
1 medium red onion, finely diced
2 cloves fresh garlic, minced
2 teaspoons natural soy sauce
3 cups cooked short grain brown rice (see note below)
½ cup shelled hempseed

Place the oil in a skillet. Add the onion and garlic and place over medium heat. When the onion begins to sizzle, add a splash of soy sauce and sauté for five minutes. Add the cooked rice and sprinkle lightly with water. Stir in the remaining soy sauce, cover, and simmer for 5 to 7 minutes. Remove from the heat and stir in the hempseed.

Note: To prepare the cooked rice, rinse 1 cup short grain brown rice and soak it in water for 1 hour. Drain and place in a heavy pot with 2 cups fresh spring or filtered water. Bring to a boil, add a pinch of sea salt, cover, and reduce the heat to low. Cook 45 to 50 minutes or until the rice has absorbed all the liquid.

There's brown rice and then there's brown rice. This version is so delicious and nutty, you'll never think of rice as "beige food" again.

Chili Corn Pie

Makes 6 to 8 servings

Crust:

½ cup yellow cornmeal

½ cup whole wheat pastry flour

¼ cup shelled hempseed, ground into a fine meal

Generous pinch of sea salt

¼ cup light-colored olive oil or avocado oil

½ cup hot spring or filtered water

Filling:

1 tablespoon extra-virgin olive oil

1 yellow onion, diced

2 cloves fresh garlic, minced

2 teaspoons chili powder

Sea salt

½ cup fresh or frozen corn kernels

½ red bell pepper, diced

2 cups cooked or canned kidney beans or black beans

½ cup shelled hempseed

¼ cup oil-cured black olives, pitted and coarsely chopped

1 cup shredded nondairy soy cheese

Here is a great casserole main course. Richly flavored, slightly spicy, and creamy rich, this Latin-style dish will win raves.

Preheat the oven to 350°F and lightly oil a standard pie plate.

Combine the cornmeal, flour, hempseed, and salt in a large bowl. Cut in the oil with a fork until the mixture is the texture of wet sand. Slowly add the water, mixing until the dough gathers into a ball. Press the dough evenly into the pie plate, pressing it up the sides and crimping the edge into a decorative rim. Bake for 10 minutes.

For the filling, place the oil in a skillet. Add the onion and garlic and place over medium heat. When the onion begins to sizzle, add the chili powder and a pinch of salt and sauté for 2 to 3 minutes. Stir in the corn and bell pepper and sauté for 2 minutes. Stir in the

beans, hempseed, and olives and sauté for 2 minutes. Season lightly with salt (remember the olives are salty). Stir in ½ cup of the soy cheese and spoon into the pie shell. Top with the remaining cheese. Bake until the cheese is bubbling and the crust is golden at the edges, about 35 minutes.

Kicharee

Makes 6 to 8 servings

2 cups dried mung beans, rinsed well and soaked for 3 hours
1 tablespoon whole coriander seeds
1½ teaspoons whole cumin seeds
8 cups spring or filtered water
1½ cups long grain brown basmati rice
2 tablespoons light-colored olive oil
2 teaspoons turmeric
1 teaspoon sea salt
¼ cup shelled hempseed

An earthy combination of mung beans, spices, and rice, this flavorful side dish is a great complement to a simple meal.

Drain the soaked beans and rinse them well. Grind the coriander and cumin in a mortar and pestle or in a spice grinder. Place a dry skillet over high heat and pan roast the coriander and cumin, stirring constantly until fragrant, about 3 minutes. Set aside.

Bring the water to a boil in a large, covered pot. Stir in the beans, basmati rice, olive oil, roasted spices, turmeric, and salt. Return to a boil. Cover and reduce the heat to low. Simmer until the beans and rice are tender and the liquid has been absorbed, about 1½ hours. Remove from the heat and fold in the hempseed.

Enchiladas

Extra-virgin olive oil

1 red bell pepper, seeded and diced

2 cloves fresh garlic, minced

1 teaspoon ground cumin

1 generous pinch of crushed red pepper flakes

Sea salt

2 to 3 stalks celery, diced

1 carrot, diced

1 (10-ounce) can diced tomatoes

1 cup cooked or canned red kidney or pinto beans

1 cup cooked or canned black beans

1 package soft corn tortillas

1½ cups shredded nondairy soy cheese

1 tablespoon minced fresh cilantro or parsley

1 cup shelled hempseed

A staple of Mexican cuisine, there are as many versions of enchiladas as there are cooks to prepare them. This delectable vegan version is easy to make. Qué bueno!

Place a small amount of olive oil in a skillet. Add the red bell pepper, garlic, cumin, and crushed red pepper flakes and place over medium heat. When the pepper begins to sizzle, add a pinch of salt and sauté until the pepper is limp. Stir in the celery and carrot, season lightly with salt, and sauté for 1 minute. Stir in the tomatoes and beans. Season to taste with salt, cover, and cook over low heat until the carrot is soft, about 15 minutes.

Preheat the oven to 350°F and lightly oil a deep-dish pie plate. Lay 3 tortillas, in overlapping circles, in the pie plate, covering the sides. Sprinkle evenly with ½ cup of the soy cheese, a sprinkle of the cilantro, ⅓ of the bean mixture, and ⅓ cup of the hempseed. Place a second layer of tortillas over the filling and sprinkle with ½ cup of soy cheese, a sprinkle of cilantro, ½ of the remaining bean mixture, and ⅓ cup of the hempseed. Sprinkle with the remaining soy cheese, bean mixture, cilantro, and hempseed. Lay the remaining tortillas over the top to cover the filling. Bake for 30 minutes or until the tortillas are browned. Allow to stand, undisturbed, for 10 minutes before slicing into wedges to serve.

Falafel

Have ready:

1½ cups Lemony HempNut Sauce, page 71

Falafel:

3 cups cooked or canned chickpeas (see note)
2 tablespoons shelled hempseed
3 cloves fresh garlic, minced
2 teaspoons ground cumin
2 teaspoons ground coriander
2 teaspoons sea salt
1 teaspoon paprika
1 teaspoon turmeric
1 or 2 scallions, minced
2 or 3 fresh parsley sprigs, minced
Whole wheat pastry flour

Another Middle Eastern tradition, falafel make the most satisfying sandwiches. You also can serve them on top of a fresh salad for a light meal. Lightly spicy, with rich flavors and a creamy sauce for dipping, these are heavenly.

Place the chickpeas, hempseed, garlic, cumin, coriander, salt, paprika, and turmeric in a food processor and purée until smooth, adding a small amount of spring or filtered water as needed to create a thick paste. Add the scallions and parsley and pulse until well combined. Transfer the mixture to a bowl and add enough flour to create a dough that holds together when formed but is not too dry. Shape into 1½-inch spheres.

Preheat the oven to 375°F and line a baking sheet with parchment. Arrange the falafel on the prepared baking sheet and bake 10 to 15 minutes or until crisp on the outside. Alternatively, deep fry the falafel in light-colored olive or avocado oil until crisp and golden brown. (Frying is the more traditional method.)

Serve the falafel stuffed into pita bread, smothered with Lemony HempNut Sauce, or as a side dish with the sauce on the side for dipping.

Note: To prepare the chickpeas, rinse 1¼ cups dried chickpeas and place them in a pressure cooker with 4 cups of water. Pressure cook for 1 hour. Alternatively, use canned organic chickpeas.

Dandelion Green Quiche

Makes 6 to 8 servings

Crust:

1 cup whole wheat pastry flour

2 tablespoons shelled hempseed

1 teaspoon ground sage

Pinch of sea salt

⅓ cup light-colored olive oil or avocado oil

Cold spring or filtered water

Filling:

Extra-virgin olive oil

1 yellow onion, diced

Sea salt

Mirin

2 to 3 cups thinly sliced dandelion greens, washed very well

1 pound extra-firm tofu

2 tablespoons sesame tahini

2 tablespoons hempseed oil

2 teaspoons shelled hempseed

Preheat the oven to 350°F and lightly oil a standard pie plate (not deep dish).

To make the crust, whisk together the flour, hempseed, sage, and salt. With a fork, cut in the olive oil until the mixture is the texture of wet sand. Add water by the tablespoon, mixing it in until the dough gathers together. Roll out the dough between two sheets of parchment to form a round about one inch larger than the pie plate. Lay the crust in the pie plate, fitting it in without stretching, allowing the excess to hang over the edge. Fold back the excess over the rim and decoratively crimp the edge by pressing it between two fingers with your thumb. Pierce the crust in several places with a fork and bake for 7 minutes. Remove from the oven and cool.

For the filling, place a small amount of olive oil in a skillet. Add the onion and place over medium heat. When the onion sizzles, add a pinch of salt and sauté for 2 to 3 minutes. Sprinkle generously with mirin and stir in the dandelion greens. Season to taste with salt. Sauté 1 to 2 minutes, just until the dandelion greens wilt. Remove from the heat and set aside.

Place the tofu, tahini, and hempseed oil in a food processor and purée until smooth, adding a small amount of water if the filling seems too thick. Transfer to a large bowl and fold in the dandelion greens. Spoon evenly into the pie shell, smoothing the top with a spatula. Sprinkle the hempseed around the rim of the quiche and bake until the edges are browned and the filling is set, about 30 minutes.

European cooking has an amazing balance to it, pairing opposing textures and flavors to create taste sensations as carefully orchestrated as any fine symphony. This creamy quiche accentuates its richness by lacing delicately bitter greens throughout.

HempNut Stuffing in Glazed
Acorn Squash Rings

Makes 6 to 8 servings

Squash Rings:

2 acorn squash, sliced into 2-inch-thick rings, seeds removed
Hempseed oil
Sea salt
Barley malt

Stuffing:

Extra-virgin olive oil
1 medium yellow onion, diced
2 cloves fresh garlic, minced
Sea salt
1 or 2 stalks celery, diced
1 carrot, diced
Grated zest of 1 fresh lemon (2 to 3 teaspoons)
1 tablespoon ground sage
Mirin
½ cup shelled hempseed
½ cup pine nuts
1 small loaf whole grain bread, cubed, dried in the oven until crisp
Spring or filtered water

Preheat the oven to 350°F. Place the squash rings on a rimmed baking sheet. Drizzle with hempseed oil, sprinkle with salt, and drizzle with barley malt. Cover tightly and bake for 30 minutes. Remove from the oven and cool.

For the stuffing, place a small amount of olive oil in a skillet. Add the onion and garlic and place over medium heat. When the onion begins to sizzle, add a pinch of salt and sauté for 1 to 2 minutes. Stir in the celery, carrot, lemon zest, and another pinch of salt. Sauté for 1 to 2 minutes. Add the sage and a generous sprinkle of mirin. Season to taste with salt and reduce the heat to low. Cook for 5 minutes, stirring occasionally. Remove from the heat and stir in the hempseed and pine nuts.

Crumble the bread cubes in a large bowl and slowly mix in just enough water to make the bread soft and moist. Stir in the sautéed vegetables and mix well to combine. Spoon the stuffing into the center of each squash ring, mounding it abundantly. Bake, uncovered, 35 to 40 minutes or until the squash is soft and the stuffing is lightly browned.

Note: Any remaining stuffing can be spooned into a lightly oiled baking dish, covered, and baked for 30 minutes. Serve it on the side.

I love to serve this dish on Thanksgiving, the holiday seemingly designed around stuffing—from the bird to ourselves. Try out this dish— no one will miss the meat.

Pan Fried Tofu and Watercress Salad

Makes 4 to 6 servings

Salad:

Avocado oil
8 to 10 ounces extra-firm tofu, cut into ½-inch-thick slices
1 carrot, cut into thin matchsticks
½ red onion, sliced into half moons
1 bunch watercress, rinsed well, tips of stems trimmed
1 tablespoon shelled hempseed, lightly pan toasted (see page 44)

Dressing:

2 tablespoons sesame tahini
1½ teaspoons natural soy sauce
1 teaspoon hempseed oil
1 teaspoon umeboshi vinegar
1 teaspoon brown rice syrup
Grated zest of 1 fresh lime (about 1 teaspoon)

Here is a great main course tofu dish. Lightly fried, the tofu is just rich enough to be satisfying without being oily. The creamy dressing, crisp fresh watercress, and crunchy hempseed strike just the right balance.

Pour 1 inch of avocado oil in a deep skillet and place over medium heat. When the oil is hot (patterns will form in the oil, known as "dancing"), fry the tofu until golden and crispy, turning once to ensure even browning. Drain on parchment or paper towels and place in a warm oven while preparing the rest of the dish.

Bring a pot of water to a boil and quickly blanch the carrot. Drain and place in a large bowl. In the same water, blanch the onion slices for 30 seconds. Drain and add to the carrot. In the same water, blanch the watercress until it just wilts, about 1 minute. Drain and cut into bite-size pieces. Mix with the other vegetables. Stir in the hempseed and arrange the mixture on a serving platter. Arrange the tofu on top.

For the dressing, whisk together all of the ingredients, adding a little water only if necessary to thin the dressing to the desired consistency. Spoon the dressing over the warm salad and serve immediately.

breads, muffins, and crackers

Whole grains are lovely, but sometimes we need a bit of luxury. Breads, muffins, and crackers made from whole grains satisfy us deeply with their crunch, moist crumb, and sensual textures.

Nothing is as inspiring or humbling as baking bread. Mixing, kneading, whisking, sifting, the fine dust of flour settling on your skin, the aroma of baking scenting the air with the intoxicating perfume of creation. Home-baked bread—whether it's a delicate, sweet quick bread or bread you knead, rise, shape, and bake into a fragrant loaf—makes everything just a little more luxurious, from sandwiches to toast.

Muffins comfort us at breakfast. Quick breads delight us as snacks and desserts. And crackers energize our parties. The added nutrition of hempseed will comfort, delight, and energize your body as well.

—Christina

Apricot Bread

Makes 1 standard loaf, 8 to 10 slices

1½ cups dried apricots
2½ cups whole wheat pastry flour
1 tablespoon aluminum-free baking powder
Generous pinch of ground cinnamon
Pinch of sea salt
½ cup light-colored olive oil or avocado oil
½ cup brown rice syrup
1 teaspoon pure vanilla extract
½ to 1 cup vanilla soymilk or rice milk
2 tablespoons shelled hempseed
Grated zest of 1 orange (about 1½ tablespoons)

Soak the apricots in warm water until tender. Drain, chop, and set aside. Preheat the oven to 350°F and lightly oil and flour a standard loaf pan.

Whisk together the flour, baking powder, cinnamon, and salt. Stir in the olive oil, rice syrup, and vanilla extract. Slowly stir in the soymilk using just enough to make a smooth batter. Fold in the hempseed, orange zest, and reserved apricots. Spoon into the prepared pan. Bake 40 to 50 minutes or until lightly browned and the top of the bread springs back to the touch. Remove from the oven and allow to stand for 10 minutes. Run a knife around the rim of the pan to loosen the bread and transfer to a cooling rack. Cool completely before slicing.

There's nothing like quick breads to make any occasion just a little special. This one is laced with dried apricots, creating a moist, delicately sweet bread that is perfect as a snack or with strong coffee or tea.

Banana Bread

Makes 1 standard loaf, 8 to 10 slices

2 cups whole wheat pastry flour
2 teaspoons aluminum-free baking powder
Generous pinch of sea salt
½ cup light-colored olive oil or avocado oil
½ cup brown rice syrup
1 teaspoon pure vanilla extract
2 ripe bananas, mashed with a fork to create a smooth paste
½ to 1 cup vanilla soymilk or rice milk
¼ cup shelled hempseed
¼ cup coarsely chopped pecans
3 tablespoons unsweetened, shredded coconut

Preheat the oven to 350°F and lightly oil and flour a standard loaf pan.

Place the flour, baking powder, and salt in a large bowl. Stir with a dry wire whisk to combine. In a separate bowl, cream together the olive oil, rice syrup, and vanilla extract using a whisk. Fold in the mashed bananas. Fold the banana mixture into the dry ingredients. Slowly add just enough soymilk to create a smooth batter. Fold in the hempseed, pecans, and coconut. Spoon into the prepared pan and bake 40 to 50 minutes or until lightly browned and the top of the bread springs back to the touch. Remove from the oven and allow to stand for 10 minutes. Run a knife around the rim of the pan to loosen the bread. Transfer the bread to a cooling rack. Serve warm or cooled.

Moist, sweet, and decadent, this simple bread is great as a snack, for breakfast, or my favorite, lightly toasted and served with nondairy ice cream as a light dessert.

Savory Cornbread

Makes 8 to 10 wedges

1½ cups whole wheat pastry flour
½ cup yellow cornmeal
3 tablespoons shelled hempseed, ground into a fine meal
2 teaspoons aluminum-free baking powder
Generous pinch of dried basil
Generous pinch of sea salt
½ cup fresh or frozen corn kernels
½ red bell pepper, minced
½ small yellow onion, finely diced
⅓ cup light-colored olive oil or avocado oil
1 tablespoon brown rice syrup
1 to 1½ cups spring or filtered water

Preheat the oven to 350°F and lightly oil and flour a 9-inch pie plate.

Whisk together the flour, cornmeal, hempseed, baking powder, basil, and salt. Add the corn, red pepper, and onion. Stir in the olive oil, rice syrup, and enough water to create a smooth batter. Spoon the batter into the prepared pie plate and bake 35 to 40 minutes or until the center of the bread springs back to the touch and the edges are lightly browned. Remove from the oven and allow to cool completely before slicing into wedges.

Variation: For a richer cornbread, substitute plain soymilk for the water.

Cornbread is perfect as an accompaniment to hearty meals such as chili, bean stews, casseroles, or roasted vegetables. It's light, so it doesn't leave you feeling heavy, but it is still satisfying and comforting.

Blue Cornbread

Makes 8 to 10 wedges

1 cup whole wheat pastry flour

¾ cup blue cornmeal

¼ cup shelled hempseed

2 teaspoons aluminum-free baking powder

1 teaspoon dried sage

Generous pinch of sea salt

⅓ cup light-colored olive oil or avocado oil

1 to 2 cups plain soymilk or rice milk

2 cups fresh or frozen corn kernels

1 teaspoon grated orange zest

Preheat the oven to 350°F and lightly oil and flour a 9-inch pie plate.

Whisk together the flour, cornmeal, hempseed, baking powder, sage, and salt. Stir in the olive oil and just enough soymilk to create a smooth batter. Fold in the corn and orange zest. Do not over mix. Spoon into the prepared pie plate and bake 35 to 40 minutes or until the center of the cornbread springs back to the touch. Remove from the oven and cool completely before slicing into wedges.

Here's a cornbread with a twist. Blue cornmeal creates a beautiful bread, rich with color and incredible flavor. I like to serve it with lighter fare, such as vegetable soups and fresh salads, to balance its hearty nature.

Whole Wheat Bread

1 quart warm spring or filtered water
7 to 8 cups whole wheat flour
¼ cup active dry yeast
1 tablespoon barley malt
½ cup shelled hempseed
1 tablespoon sea salt
¼ cup light-colored olive oil or avocado oil
4 tablespoons brown rice syrup

Baking bread can be humbling, as we discover that nature has her own mind and we are subject to her whim. But hang in there. Baking bread is worth the humility.

To make the sponge, combine the warm water, 1 cup of the flour, the yeast, and barley malt in a large bowl. Cover tightly with plastic wrap and set aside to rise in a warm place until doubled, about 1 hour. Stir down, cover, and set aside to rise again for about 30 minutes.

Stir into the sponge 2½ cups of the flour, the hempseed, and salt. Stir in the olive oil and rice syrup and mix well. Add the remaining flour, by the cup, to create a smooth, slightly sticky dough. (You will have some flour left over.)

Flour a dry work surface and turn the dough onto the flour. Knead about 10 minutes, slowly adding flour as necessary to create a smooth, elastic dough. (Do not add too much flour, as it will make for dry bread.) Divide the dough into 3 equal pieces. Shape into loaves and place on floured baking sheets or baking stones. Cover with a damp towel and place in a warm, dry place until doubled in size, about 45 minutes.

Preheat the oven to 350°F and bake 45 to 50 minutes or until the loaves sound hollow when tapped. Cool before slicing.

Note: To create a crisp outer crust, fill a spritz bottle with water and spray the loaves and the inside of the oven every 5 minutes for the first 15 minutes of bake time.

Variation: To create a sourdough bread, replace the yeasted sponge with 2 cups sourdough starter.

Bright Red Deadhead Bread

Makes 2 to 3 small loaves

3 tablespoons active dry yeast
2½ cups warm spring or filtered water
⅓ cup barley malt
2 cups cooked puréed beets
½ cup hempseed oil
1 tablespoon sea salt
2½ cups semolina flour (plus additional for dusting)
2½ cups whole wheat flour
½ cup shelled hempseed

This richly colored bread is delicately sweet and satisfying. The minerals from the beets join with the essential fatty acids and complete protein of hempseed to make bread that is more than just delicious.

Place the yeast in a large bowl. Add ½ cup of the warm water and 1 teaspoon of the barley malt. Set aside for 5 minutes. Stir in the remaining water, barley malt, puréed beets, hempseed oil, and salt. By the cup, mix in the flours, starting with the semolina. The dough will gather together and become sticky and cohesive. Dust a dry surface with semolina flour and turn out the dough. Knead 5 to 7 minutes or until the dough is smooth and elastic, adding semolina flour as needed. (Do not add too much flour, as it will make for dry bread.) During the last 2 or 3 minutes of kneading, spread the hempseed on the work surface and knead it into the dough.

Shape the dough into 2 to 3 small loaves and transfer to a semolina-dusted baking sheet or baking stone. Cover with a damp kitchen towel and set aside to rise in a warm place until doubled in size, about 45 minutes.

Preheat the oven to 375°F and bake the loaves for 45 to 50 minutes or until they sound hollow when tapped.

Note: The kneading process naturally dries the dough, so add flour slowly and in small amounts. This will ensure that your bread will not be tough and dry. Proper kneading is key to the bread.

Lemony-Hempseed Pound Cake

Makes 8 to 10 servings

Pound Cake:

2½ cups whole wheat pastry flour

2 tablespoons shelled hempseed

Grated zest of 2 fresh lemons (4 to 6 teaspoons)

1 tablespoon baking powder

¼ teaspoon sea salt

½ cup light-colored olive oil

½ cup brown rice syrup

Juice of 2 fresh lemons (about 6 tablespoons)

1 teaspoon pure vanilla extract

½ to 1 cup Eden Rice & Soy Blend or vanilla soymilk or rice milk

Lemon Glaze:

½ cup brown rice syrup

Grated zest of 1 lemon (2 to 3 teaspoons)

This cake is rich and moist, with just a touch of lemony satisfaction. It's the perfect dessert after a hearty meal.

Preheat the oven to 325°F and lightly oil and flour a standard loaf or small Bundt pan.

Combine the flour, hempseed, lemon zest, baking powder, and salt. Whisk briskly. Stir in the olive oil, rice syrup, lemon juice, and vanilla extract. Slowly add the milk to create a smooth batter. Spoon into the prepared loaf pan. Bake 35 to 40 minutes or until the center of the loaf springs back to the touch or a toothpick inserted near the center comes out clean. Remove from the oven and allow to cool for 10 minutes. Run a sharp knife around the rim of the pan to loosen the cake. Invert the cake onto a wire rack and let cool completely.

To prepare the glaze, heat the rice syrup and lemon zest until it foams. Immediately spoon over the cake.

Crackers

Makes 20 to 24 crackers

1 cup whole wheat pastry flour
1 cup whole wheat flour
1½ teaspoons aluminum-free baking powder
1 teaspoon sea salt
¼ cup plain soy yogurt
1 tablespoon light-colored olive oil or avocado oil
2 tablespoons shelled hempseed
Cold spring or filtered water

Preheat the oven to 350°F and line a baking sheet with parchment.

Place the flours, baking powder, and salt in a large bowl and whisk briskly to combine. Stir in the yogurt and olive oil and mix well to create a stiff dough. Fold in the hempseed. Slowly add just enough water to create a soft, smooth dough (about ½ cup, but add by tablespoons). On a dry work surface, roll the dough between two sheets of parchment until it is about ⅛ inch thick. Using a 2-inch cookie cutter or jar lid, cut round crackers, re-rolling the excess dough until all of it is used. Arrange the crackers on the prepared baking sheet. Decoratively pierce each cracker with a fork in several places. Bake 10 to 15 minutes or until golden brown. Remove from the oven and cool completely on the baking sheet. The crackers will crisp as they cool.

Variation: If you prefer square crackers, cut the dough with a scalloped ravioli cutter or a knife.

You can buy crackers or you can make these spectacular ones yourself. Trust me, one batch of these and you'll say goodbye to packaged crackers for good.

Apple Muffins

Makes about 1 dozen muffins

1 cup whole wheat pastry flour
1 cup semolina flour
3 tablespoons shelled hempseed
2 teaspoons aluminum-free baking powder
Generous pinch of sea salt
Generous pinch of ground cinnamon
Scant pinch of ground nutmeg
⅓ cup light-colored olive oil or avocado oil
⅓ cup brown rice syrup
½ to 1 cup vanilla soymilk or rice milk
1 cup finely diced Granny Smith apple (do not peel)
¼ cup finely chopped pecans

Preheat the oven to 350°F and lightly oil a 12-cup standard muffin tin.

Place the flours, hempseed, baking powder, salt, cinnamon, and nutmeg in a large bowl. Whisk until well combined. Stir in the olive oil and rice syrup. Slowly add just enough soymilk to create a smooth batter. Fold in the apple and pecans. Spoon the batter evenly into the prepared muffin cups. Bake 30 to 35 minutes or until the center of the muffins spring back to the touch. Remove from the oven and allow to cool completely before removing from the tin.

Variation: You may substitute any firm fruit for the apple, such as pears, apricots, peaches, or mangoes.

These muffins make the ideal autumn snack, when apples are at their sweet and crispy best. Delicately sweet, with a hint of cinnamon, the perfume of these muffins will have your loved ones rushing to the table.

Rosemary Muffins

Makes about 1 dozen muffins

2 cups whole wheat pastry flour
½ cup semolina flour
2 tablespoons shelled hempseed
1 tablespoon aluminum-free baking powder
2 teaspoons ground rosemary
Pinch of sea salt
½ cup hempseed oil or light-colored olive oil
2 tablespoons brown rice syrup
½ to 1 cup plain soymilk or rice milk

Preheat the oven to 350°F and lightly oil a 12-cup standard muffin tin.

Whisk together the flours, hempseed, baking powder, rosemary, and salt. Stir in the hempseed oil and rice syrup. Slowly add just enough soymilk to create a smooth batter. Spoon evenly into the prepared muffin cups and bake 30 to 35 minutes or until the tops spring back to the touch and the muffins are golden brown.

Savory muffins are ideal at a brunch, with soup for a light lunch, or in place of bread at any meal. Laced with fragrant rosemary, these muffins are not only delicious, they are good for our tummies, because rosemary aids in digestion.

Cherry Scones

1½ cups whole wheat pastry flour
1½ cups semolina flour
½ cup shelled hempseed
1 tablespoon aluminum-free baking powder
1 teaspoon baking soda
1 teaspoon ground cinnamon
Generous pinch of sea salt
⅔ cup brown rice syrup
⅓ cup light-colored olive oil or avocado oil
1 teaspoon pure vanilla extract
1 to 2 cups plain soy yogurt
1 cup pitted fresh or frozen cherries, coarsely chopped

Preheat the oven to 350°F and line a baking sheet with parchment.

Place the flours, hempseed, baking powder, baking soda, cinnamon, and salt in a large bowl and whisk until well combined. Stir in the rice syrup, olive oil, and vanilla extract. Slowly add just enough soy yogurt to make a soft, thick, formable dough. Fold in the chopped cherries.

Place ½-cup portions of the dough on the lined baking sheet. With moist fingers, flatten each scone slightly or form it into triangular shapes. Bake until golden at the edges and firm to the touch, about 20 minutes.

Variation: You can vary the fruit—blueberries, peaches, or raspberries are great in these scones.

Scones are lovely. They are a bit heartier than muffins and cookies but lighter than bread—perfect for a light afternoon snack with your sweetie. And these scones, lush with fresh cherries, have a romantic sensuality.

Golden Biscuits

Makes about 24 biscuits

1 cup whole wheat pastry flour
½ cup semolina flour
2 teaspoons aluminum-free baking powder
Generous pinch of sea salt
⅓ cup light-colored olive oil or avocado oil
2 tablespoons barley malt
1 cup winter squash (butternut is best)
   or carrot purée (see note below)
Plain soymilk or rice milk
¼ cup shelled hempseed

I love to serve these biscuits with hot soup or a hearty stew on a chilly winter night. Their rich golden color is so warming it's easy to overlook their delicate sweet flavor and tender, moist texture.

Preheat the oven to 350°F and line a baking sheet with parchment.

Place the flours, baking powder, and salt in a large bowl. Stir with a whisk to combine. Stir in the olive oil and barley malt. Fold in the squash purée, mixing to create a soft, formable dough, adding soymilk only if needed to make the dough moist enough. Fold in the hempseed.

On a lightly floured surface, press the dough into a rectangle about ¾ inch thick. Using a 2-inch biscuit cutter or jar lid, cut the biscuits, re-pressing the excess until all the dough is used. Arrange the biscuits on the lined baking sheet about 1 inch apart. Bake for 15 to 20 minutes or until slightly puffed and browned at the edges.

Notes: • To make the squash purée, peel and cube one quarter of a medium-size squash or one half of a small squash, and stew it with very little water until the squash is quite soft. Drain any cooking liquid and mash until smooth. For carrot purée, dice and cook 3 to 4 carrots until soft, and purée.

• When cutting biscuits, take care to cut straight down. Do not twist the cutter, as this will take air from the batter, resulting in heavy, dense biscuits.

Hip2Hemp Snack Bars

Makes about 20 bars

1½ cups rolled oats
¼ cup shelled hempseed
¼ cup sunflower seeds
¼ cup coarsely chopped pecans
⅛ teaspoon sea salt
Generous pinch of ground cinnamon
⅓ cup brown rice syrup
¼ cup hempseed oil
½ teaspoon pure vanilla extract

Preheat the oven to 350°F and line a baking sheet with parchment.

Heat a dry skillet over medium heat. Stir in the oats and pan toast until lightly browned. Transfer to a bowl and stir in the hempseed, sunflower seeds, pecans, salt, and cinnamon. Stir in the rice syrup, hempseed oil, and vanilla extract, and mix until the batter holds together. On the baking sheet, form the mixture into an 8 x 10-inch rectangle, about ¼ inch thick. Bake 12 to 15 minutes or until the edges are lightly browned. Allow to cool for 5 minutes. Using a fork, split the rectangle into bars.

Easy, delicious, and packed with nutrients, these incredible bars are simply the greatest snack.

Scallion-Hempseed Mini-Muffins

Makes about 24 mini-muffins
or 12 standard muffins

7 tablespoons light-colored olive oil or avocado oil
1 bunch scallions, rinsed and thinly sliced
1 cup semolina flour
1 cup whole wheat pastry flour
¼ cup cornmeal
¼ cup plus 2 teaspoons shelled hempseed
2 teaspoons baking powder
⅛ teaspoon sea salt
¼ cup brown rice syrup
2½ cups plain soymilk or rice milk

Preheat the oven to 350°F and lightly oil a 24-cup miniature muffin tin or 12-cup standard tin (you may also use foil cups or paper liners).

Place 3 tablespoons of the olive oil in a skillet. Add the scallions and place over medium heat. Sauté until bright green and limp, about 1 minute. Set aside to cool.

Combine the flours and cornmeal, ¼ cup of the hempseed, the baking powder, and salt in a large bowl. Stir in the remaining 4 tablespoons of oil and the rice syrup. Slowly add the soymilk, using just enough to make a thick batter. Fold in the sautéed scallions.

Divide the batter evenly among the muffin cups. Sprinkle the tops with the remaining 2 teaspoons of hempseed. Bake 25 to 30 minutes or until golden and firm to the touch. Cool for about 10 minutes before carefully removing the muffins from the tin. Serve warm or at room temperature.

Cornmeal, with its characteristic coarseness, helps the body to digest the flour. The scallions provide a light, uplifting energy to prevent the heaviness often associated with flour products, and the hempseed provides essential fatty acids and protein.

desserts

I read an interview with the great pastry chef Maida Haetter (one of my personal heroes) and she was asked if she enjoyed cooking as much as baking. She answered that cooking was just great, like the warm-up to the baseball game. I say: Hear, hear!

When I changed my eating patterns to create a healthier life, my greatest fear was that there would be no dessert. I thought I would be doomed to a grim existence of tofu and bean sprouts (not that they don't have a place in my heart)—but dessert is dessert.

Oh, I tried healthy desserts. You know the ones—muffins with the texture of dry sand, cookies that could double as hockey pucks, cakes that serve better as doorstops or paperweights. And since I couldn't face the possibility of life without desserts, I decided to get creative. What I discovered was that the ingredients had changed, but the techniques were the same. Equipped with years of experience, I took whole grain flours, excellent oils, natural sweeteners, soy, grain and nut milks, and hempseed and oil and began creating desserts as delicious and decadent as their less-than-healthy counterparts.

Dessert relaxes us, makes us happy, and helps us to celebrate special and not-so-special occasions. However, there's no place in a healthy diet for white sugar, white flour, butter, eggs, and all the many other ingredients that have given dessert a bad reputation.

The essential fatty acids and protein in these dessert recipes leave us feeling satisfied, so we are less tempted to binge or crave harmful foods, and we may actually be content with smaller portions. Ahh, nutrition so delicious! Remember, a bit of sweet makes life all the sweeter.

—Christina

Pie Crust

Makes 1 crust (8 to 10 servings)

1 cup whole wheat pastry flour
¼ cup semolina flour
2 tablespoons shelled hempseed
Pinch of sea salt
⅓ cup light-colored olive oil or avocado oil
Spring or filtered water

Combine the flours, hempseed, and salt in a bowl. Using a fork, cut in the olive oil until the mixture is the texture of wet sand. Slowly stir in just enough water so the dough gathers together. Roll out between two sheets parchment to form a round that is 1 inch larger than the pie plate. The crust should be thin and evenly rolled. Lay the crust over a pie plate, fitting it in without stretching. Allow the excess crust to hang over the rim of the pie plate.

Here is a basic pie crust to fill all your pie baking needs. The addition of hempseed helps to hold the crust together, while the oil in the seeds makes the crust light and flaky.

Dutch Apple Pie

Makes 1 pie (8 to 10 slices)

Have ready:

1 Pie Crust, page 145

Filling:

2 tablespoons light-colored olive oil or avocado oil
4 tablespoons brown rice syrup
6 to 8 Gala, Cortland, or other crisp apples, peeled, cored, and thinly sliced
Grated zest of 1 fresh lemon (2 to 3 teaspoons)
Generous pinch of sea salt
Generous pinch of ground cinnamon
2 tablespoons arrowroot

Topping:

1 cup pecans, coarsely chopped
¼ cup whole wheat pastry flour
3 tablespoons brown rice syrup
Light-colored olive oil or avocado oil

This homey, cozy dessert just perfect for those nights when you want a little something special for curling up on the sofa with your sweetie.

Preheat the oven to 325°F. Prepare the pie crust according to the recipe directions and set aside.

For the filling, place the olive oil and rice syrup in a deep skillet over medium heat. Stir in the apples, lemon zest, salt, and cinnamon. Sauté the apples 5 to 6 minutes or until just limp. Dissolve the arrowroot in 3 to 4 tablespoons of cold water and stir into the apples to create a thin glaze. Spoon the apples evenly into the pie crust.

To prepare the topping, combine the pecans, flour, rice syrup, and just enough olive oil to create a crumbly texture. Sprinkle over the apple filling, covering it completely. Place the pie on a baking sheet and bake until the topping is browned and the apples are tender, about 1 hour.

HempNut Cookbook

Baked Apples

3 large, ripe apples (do not peel)
⅓ cup coarsely chopped pecans
⅓ cup shelled hempseed
3 tablespoons organic raisins
1 teaspoon pure vanilla extract
½ teaspoon ground cinnamon
½ teaspoon ground cardamom
3 tablespoons brown rice syrup
3 tablespoons unsweetened apricot preserves

Preheat the oven to 375°F. Using a melon baller or small spoon, core the apples and remove the seeds, but do not go through the apple. Leave the bottom intact. Arrange the apples in a shallow baking dish, standing on their bottom sides.

Combine the pecans, hempseed, raisins, vanilla extract, cinnamon, and cardamom. Mix well and spoon abundantly into each apple, filling it completely. Whisk together the rice syrup and preserves. Spoon over the apples. Pour ¼ inch of water in the bottom of the baking dish. Bake, uncovered, 40 to 45 minutes or until the apples pierce easily with a fork. Serve hot.

Juicy baked apples are as delightful as the season they herald—autumn. Filled with sweet dried fruit, nuts, seeds, and spices to enhance the natural succulence of the apples, this dessert is as enchanting as it is easy to make.

Blueberry Apple Cobbler

Makes 6 to 8 servings

Topping:

4 cups rolled oats
1 cup whole wheat pastry flour
½ cup coarsely chopped pecans
3 tablespoons shelled hempseed
Pinch of sea salt
⅓ cup light-colored olive oil or avocado oil
⅓ cup brown rice syrup
Vanilla soymilk or rice milk

Cobbler:

6 small Granny Smith apples, diced (do not peel)
6 cups fresh blueberries, rinsed well
⅓ cup brown rice syrup
¼ cup light-colored olive oil or avocado oil
3 tablespoons arrowroot powder
¼ teaspoon ground cardamom
¼ teaspoon ground cinnamon
¼ teaspoon ground anise
Generous pinch of sea salt

Serve this scrumptious fruit cobbler on those occasions when only something comforting will do.

Preheat the oven to 350°F and lightly oil a 9 x 13-inch glass baking dish.

For the topping, combine the oats, flour, pecans, hempseed, and salt in a bowl. Stir in the olive oil and rice syrup and mix until crumbly, adding a small amount of soymilk if needed to create the texture you desire. (More soymilk will create a cake-like topping, while less will result in a streusel topping.)

For the cobbler, combine the apples and berries in a large bowl. Mix in the remaining ingredients, and stir to coat. Spoon the fruit evenly into the prepared baking dish and crumble the topping over the surface of the fruit, covering it completely.

Bake 35 to 40 minutes or until the filling is bubbling and the topping has lightly browned.

Vanilla HempNut Cake

Makes 6 to 8 servings

2 cups whole wheat pastry flour
½ cup semolina flour
2½ teaspoons aluminum-free baking powder
⅛ teaspoon sea salt
½ cup light-colored olive oil or avocado oil
½ cup brown rice syrup
1 teaspoon pure vanilla extract
½ to 1 cup vanilla soymilk or rice milk
2 tablespoons shelled hempseed

Preheat the oven to 350°F and lightly oil and flour a standard Bundt pan, round cake pan, or loaf pan.

Whisk together the flours, baking powder, and salt. Stir in the olive oil, rice syrup, and vanilla extract. Slowly stir in just enough soymilk to create a smooth, satiny batter. Fold in the hempseed.

Spoon the batter evenly into the prepared pan. Bake 35 to 40 minutes or until the top of the cake springs back to the touch or a toothpick inserted comes out clean. Remove from the oven and allow to cool for 5 minutes before removing from the pan. Serve glazed, frosted, or with your favorite fruit.

This vanilla cake will take you anywhere your dessert imagination wants to go. Use it as the basic recipe for building your repertoire—muffins, cupcakes, cakes, loaves—and any variation you can envision.

Apple Cake

Cake:

2 cups whole wheat pastry flour

½ cup semolina flour

2½ teaspoons aluminum-free baking powder

1 teaspoon ground cinnamon

1 teaspoon ground cardamom

⅛ teaspoon sea salt

½ cup light-colored olive oil or avocado oil

½ cup brown rice syrup

½ to 1 cup vanilla soymilk or rice milk

2 cups peeled and diced apples (Granny Smith or Macintosh are best)

3 tablespoons shelled hempseed

Cinnamon Glaze:

1 cup brown rice syrup

Grated zest of 1 fresh lemon (2 to 3 teaspoons)

1 teaspoon pure vanilla extract

½ teaspoon ground cinnamon

Pinch of sea salt

Moist, delicately sweet, and scented with the perfume of autumn, this tender cake is a delightful ending to any cool-weather feast.

Preheat the oven to 350°F and lightly oil and flour a standard Bundt pan.

Whisk together the flours, baking powder, cinnamon, cardamom, and salt. Stir in the olive oil and rice syrup. Slowly mix in just enough soymilk to form a smooth, satiny batter. Fold in the apples and hempseed. Spoon evenly into the prepared pan and bake 35 to 40 minutes or until the center of the cake springs back to the touch or a toothpick inserted comes out clean. Remove from the oven and allow to stand for 5 minutes before inverting the cake onto a wire rack. Cool completely before glazing.

For the glaze, place all the ingredients in a sauce pan and bring to a foaming boil. Slip a piece of parchment paper under the wire rack holding the cake. Spoon the glaze over the cake, repeating for several coats until all the glaze is used.

Real Fruit Cake

Makes 8 to 10 servings

1 cup chopped pitted dates
1 cup dried apples, coarsely chopped
1 cup dried apricots, coarsely chopped
3 tablespoons shelled hempseed
1½ cups whole wheat pastry flour
½ cup semolina flour
2 teaspoons aluminum-free baking powder
¼ teaspoon sea salt
¼ teaspoon ground cinnamon
¼ teaspoon powdered ginger
½ cup light-colored olive oil or avocado oil
½ cup brown rice syrup
1 teaspoon pure vanilla extract
½ to 1 cup vanilla soymilk or rice milk

I know what you're thinking—fruit cake? Like the joke? Well, don't panic. Our version is tender, moist, and laced with dried fruit, creating a richly flavored dessert that is sure to please.

Preheat the oven to 325°F and lightly oil and flour a standard loaf pan. Combine the dates, apples, apricots, and hempseed in a bowl and set aside.

Whisk together the flours, baking powder, salt, cinnamon, and ginger in a large bowl. Stir in the olive oil, rice syrup, and vanilla extract. Slowly stir in just enough soymilk to create a thick batter. Fold in the fruit and hempseed. Spoon evenly into the prepared loaf pan. Bake 35 to 45 minutes or until the top of the cake springs back to the touch or a toothpick inserted comes out clean. Remove from the oven and cool for 10 minutes before removing from the pan.

Note: This cake will store well if wrapped tightly and stored in a cool place. You may also soak it in rum before storing, as tradition dictates.

Baklava

⅔ cup light-colored olive oil or avocado oil

1 cup brown rice syrup

½ cup barley malt

¼ cup rose water or apple juice

1 tablespoon grated orange zest

1 teaspoon ground cinnamon

½ teaspoon ground cardamom

2 cups ground blanched almonds

½ cup shelled hempseed

1 box whole wheat phyllo, thawed in the refrigerator

Preheat the oven to 350°F and lightly oil a 9 x 13-inch casserole dish. Place the olive oil in a small bowl for brushing. Make a syrup by whisking together the rice syrup, barley malt, rose water, orange zest, cinnamon, and cardamom. In a separate bowl, combine the almonds and hempseed.

Lay 3 sheets of the phyllo on the bottom of the prepared casserole dish. Brush lightly with oil. Sprinkle half the nut mixture over the phyllo and spoon some syrup over top. Lay 3 more sheets of phyllo on top, brush with oil, and sprinkle with the remaining nuts and hempseed. Spoon some syrup over the top. Lay another 3 sheets of phyllo on top. Mix together the remaining oil with the syrup and pour over the entire dish. Bake until the top is quite crisp and browned, about 45 minutes. Cool slightly before slicing into diamond-shaped squares.

The Middle East has given us so many wonderful dishes, it's hard to keep track. But of all the delicious options, none equal this flaky, nut filled, sweet pastry.

Spice Cookies

Makes 18 to 24 cookies

1⅓ cups whole wheat pastry flour
⅓ cup semolina flour
1 teaspoon non-aluminum baking powder
¼ teaspoon ground cinnamon
¼ teaspoon ground cardamom
¼ teaspoon ground anise seed
⅛ teaspoon sea salt
⅓ cup shelled hempseed
⅓ cup light-colored olive or avocado oil
⅓ cup brown rice syrup
1 teaspoon pure vanilla extract
Vanilla soymilk or rice milk

Preheat the oven to 350°F and line a baking sheet with parchment. Whisk together the flours, baking powder, cinnamon, cardamom, anise seed, and salt. Stir in the hempseed. Stir in the olive oil, rice syrup, and vanilla extract and mix well. Slowly add just enough soymilk to make a thick batter. Drop by tablespoons onto the prepared baking sheet, leaving about 1 inch between them. Bake 18 to 20 minutes or until lightly browned at the edges. Remove from the oven and allow to cool for 5 minutes on the hot baking sheet before removing to a wire rack to cool completely.

Spice cookies are as cozy as cookies come—
delicately sweet, with a hint of spice to
make them tingle on our tongue.

Chocolate Chip Cookies

Makes about 24 cookies

2½ cups whole wheat pastry flour
1 teaspoon baking powder
Pinch of sea salt
Pinch of ground cinnamon
½ cup brown rice syrup
⅓ cup extra-virgin olive oil
2 tablespoons hempseed oil
1 tablespoon grain coffee granules
½ to 2 cups Eden Rice & Soy Blend
1 cup nondairy grain-sweetened chocolate chips
¼ cup shelled hempseed
¼ cup coarsely chopped pecans
¼ cup unsweetened shredded coconut

Preheat the oven to 350°F and line a baking sheet with parchment. Mix together the flour, baking powder, salt, and cinnamon. Mix in the rice syrup, olive oil, and hempseed oil. Dissolve the grain coffee in ½ cup of the Eden Blend, and stir it into the flour mixture. Slowly add more Eden Blend as needed to make a soft cookie dough. Fold in the chocolate chips, hempseed, pecans, and coconut.

Drop by tablespoons onto the prepared baking sheet, leaving 1 inch in between the cookies. Gently press with your hands to flatten slightly. Bake 18 to 20 minutes or until the cookies are lightly browned but not hard. Remove from the oven and immediately transfer to a wire cooling rack.

What cookbook would be complete without a chocolate chip cookie recipe? Adding hempseed and oil ratchets up the flavor in these amazing cookies and packs them with nutrients. Chocolate and healthy ingredients? You can have your cake and eat it after all!

Hip Squares

1 cup rolled oats
1 cup raw pumpkin seeds
½ cup coarsely chopped pecans
2 cups brown rice syrup
½ cup shelled hempseed
2 tablespoons sesame tahini
Pinch of sea salt
Scant pinch of ground cinnamon

Preheat the oven to 325°F and lightly oil an 8-inch square baking dish. Spread the oats, pumpkin seeds, and pecan pieces on a baking sheet and bake for 20 minutes, stirring frequently to prevent over-browning. Transfer to a medium bowl. Combine the rice syrup, hempseed, tahini, salt, and cinnamon in a saucepan and place over medium heat. Cook and stir for 5 to 7 minutes to develop the flavors. Spoon the mixture over the toasted oats, pumpkin seeds, and nuts and mix well to combine. Transfer to the prepared baking dish and press gently so the mixture is evenly distributed. Cool for 5 minutes and then cut with a moist knife into 2-inch squares.

These great little snack squares are perfect for packing in lunch boxes.

Biscotti

Makes 24 to 30 biscotti

Biscotti:

1⅔ cups whole wheat pastry flour

⅓ cup semolina flour

2 teaspoons aluminum-free baking powder

Generous pinch of sea salt

Scant pinch of ground cinnamon

2 cups brown rice syrup

⅓ cup hempseed oil

1 teaspoon pure vanilla extract

Vanilla soymilk or rice milk

2 tablespoons hempseed

2 tablespoons coarsely chopped walnuts

Ganache (optional):

1 cup nondairy grain-sweetened chocolate chips

¼ cup vanilla soymilk or rice milk

2 teaspoons brown rice syrup

Biscotti are delicious Italian cookies with a crisp, crumbly texture that comes from the many eggs traditionally used in the recipe. So as vegans, do we face a life without them? Not as long as we have hempseed and oil. The albumin-like protein in hemp binds the cookies and gives them the texture that has made them everybody's favorite treat to dip into espresso.

Preheat the oven to 350°F and line a baking sheet with parchment. Whisk together the flours, baking powder, salt, and cinnamon. Stir in the rice syrup, hempseed oil, and vanilla extract. Slowly stir in just enough soymilk to create a soft, pliable dough. Knead 2 to 3 times to hold the dough together. Fold in the hempseed and walnut pieces and mix well to incorporate them into the dough. Divide the dough in half and, using moist hands, form each half into a long log about 10 inches long and 2 inches in wide. Place on the prepared baking sheet and bake 30 to 35 minutes or until the top of each log is firm. Remove from the oven and allow to stand on the baking sheet for 2 minutes. Carefully transfer each log to a dry cutting board. Using a sharp, serrated knife, slice each log into ¾-inch-thick diagonal slices. Lay the slices, cut-side up, on the baking sheet and bake for 3 minutes. Turn the slices over and bake for 3 to 4 minutes longer or until the

cookies are crisp. Remove from the oven and allow to cool completely on the baking sheet.

Once the biscotti have cooled completely, make the optional ganache. Place the chocolate chips in a heat-resistant bowl. Combine the soymilk and rice syrup in a small saucepan and bring to a rolling boil over high heat. Pour over the chocolate and whisk to form a smooth, shiny ganache.

Dip one half of each cookie into the ganache and place on parchment. Allow to stand until the glaze sets. You can also place the ganache in a squeeze bottle and drizzle it over each cookie.

Goo Balls

Makes 10 to 12 servings

1 cup nondairy grain-sweetened chocolate chips
1 cup almond butter
1 cup brown rice syrup
1 teaspoon pure vanilla extract
¼ teaspoon ground cinnamon
3 cups crisped brown rice cereal
⅓ cup shelled hempseed

Place the chocolate chips, almond butter, rice syrup, vanilla extract, and cinnamon in a saucepan over medium-low heat. Cook, stirring constantly, until the mixture loosens and turns creamy. Quickly fold in the rice cereal and hempseed. With moist hands, form the mixture into 1-inch spheres. Set aside until firm.

Chocolaty, rich, and deeply satisfying, this dessert is so easy to make you'll want it every day.

Rice Pudding

Makes 4 to 6 servings

3 cups almond amasake
3 cups vanilla soymilk or rice milk
1 cup arborio rice (do not rinse)
¾ cup organic raisins
2 tablespoons shelled hempseed
1 cinnamon stick
Grated zest of ½ fresh orange (about 2¼ teaspoons)
1 teaspoon ground cardamom
1 vanilla bean, split down the middle, pulp removed
Pinch of salt
¼ cup unsweetened shredded coconut, lightly toasted (for garnish)

Place all the ingredients, except the coconut, in a saucepan and mix well. Place over medium heat and bring to a boil, stirring constantly. Reduce the heat to very low and cook, stirring occasionally, until creamy. This could take up to 2 hours (the longer the better). If the liquid absorbs too quickly, simply add more soymilk or amasake. When the pudding is ready, remove and discard the cinnamon stick. Spoon into individual cups and garnish with the toasted coconut.

Note: To toast the coconut, preheat the oven to 350°F and spread the coconut on a dry baking sheet. Place in the oven for 2 to 3 minutes or until it turns light golden. Be very attentive, as coconut burns quickly.

I love rice pudding—it's so creamy, sweet, and comforting, while still being rich enough to seem decadent.

Banana Pops

⅓ cup unsweetened cocoa powder
2 tablespoons hot spring or filtered water
2 teaspoons brown rice syrup
4 ripe bananas
4 Popsicle sticks
½ cup shelled hempseed

Make a coating by mixing the cocoa powder, hot water, and rice syrup to form a smooth, creamy paste. Take care not to thin the cocoa too much. Insert a Popsicle stick into each banana and dip the banana into the syrup, coating it completely. Roll the coated bananas in the hempseed. Place on wax paper and freeze until firm. Eat while still frozen.

Banana pops are a great substitute for ice cream. Hot summer weather makes us crave sweet, cold treats, and these are delicious and creamy, without any dairy fat.

Caramel Popcorn

½ cup brown rice syrup
½ cup barley malt
1 tablespoon hempseed oil
Pinch of sea salt
4 quarts of popped organic popcorn
½ cup shelled hempseed

Combine the rice syrup, barley malt, hempseedoil, and salt in a saucepan and place over medium heat. Cook, stirring frequently, until the mixture develops a high foam.

Place the popcorn in a large bowl and pour the hot syrup over it. Mix well to coat evenly. Stir in the hempseed. Set aside for about 10 minutes to allow the glaze to harden.

Just like the sticky sweet caramel corn we get at the movies, but this version won't rot your teeth!

Baked Bananas

Makes 8 servings

4 ripe bananas
⅓ cup barley malt
1 tablespoon light-colored olive oil or avocado oil
½ cup shelled hempseed

Preheat the oven to 350°F. Peel the bananas and slice each of them lengthwise and crosswise, making 16 pieces. Layer one half of the bananas in a shallow 1-quart baking dish. Whisk together the barley malt and olive oil. Spoon one half over the bananas and sprinkle half of the hempseed over top. Cover with the remaining bananas. Spoon the remaining barley malt mixture and hempseed over top. Bake for 20 minutes. Then place under the broiler for 2 to 3 minutes or until the topping is bubbling and lightly browned.

Variation: Serve the Baked Bananas on a pool of delicate raspberry or mango sauce.

Add a bit of the tropics to your table with this light yet decadently rich dessert.

Stuffed Dates

Makes 6 to 12 servings

6 Medjool dates, sliced lengthwise and pits removed
⅓ cup shelled hempseed, ground into a fine meal
2 tablespoons brown rice syrup
12 whole almonds

Place the sliced dates open-side up on parchment paper. Combine the hempseed with the rice syrup to form a thick paste. Spoon into each date half and place one whole almond on top, pressing it in gently.

Simple, sweet and satisfying. Need we say more?

Chocolate Torte

Makes 8 to 10 servings

Have ready:

1 Pie Crust, page 145

Filling:

2 cups almond flavored amasake

1 cup vanilla soymilk

4 tablespoons brown rice syrup

1 teaspoon pure vanilla extract

3 tablespoons kuzu or arrowroot powder, dissolved in a
    small amount of cold water

2 cups nondairy grain-sweetened chocolate chips

1 cup lightly toasted slivered almonds

1 pint fresh raspberries (for garnish)

Want a dessert that's about as decadent and sinfully delicious as you can imagine? Look no further!

Preheat the oven to 350°F and prepare the pie crust according to the directions. Bake until lightly browned and fully cooked, about 17 minutes. Remove from the oven and cool completely.

Combine the amasake, soymilk, rice syrup, and vanilla extract in a saucepan and place over low heat. When the mixture is warmed through, stir in the dissolved kuzu and cook and stir 3 to 4 minutes or until the amasake thickens. Reserve 1 cup. Spoon the remaining amasake pudding evenly into the pie shell.

Stir the chocolate chips into the reserved cup of pudding, whisking until smooth and satiny. Sprinkle the slivered almonds evenly over the pudding in the pie shell and spread the chocolate topping carefully over the entire surface of the pie. Arrange the raspberries decoratively around the rim of the pie, pressing them gently into the chocolate. Chill the pie until it is set before serving.

Variation: If you prefer, substitute cocoa powder for the semolina flour in the crust to create a chocolate pie crust.

Tofu Cheesecake

Makes 8 to 10 servings

Crust:

10 unsweetened graham crackers
¼ cup shelled hempseed
Pinch of sea salt
3 tablespoons spring or filtered water
2 tablespoons light-colored olive oil or avocado oil
2 tablespoons brown rice syrup

Filling:

2 pounds soft tofu, boiled 5 minutes, drained, and cooled
⅔ cup brown rice syrup
½ cup light-colored olive oil or avocado oil
3 tablespoons fresh lemon juice
1 tablespoon pure vanilla extract
½ teaspoon sea salt

Topping:

2 cups frozen raspberries, blueberries, or strawberries
3 tablespoons brown rice syrup
Grated zest of 1 fresh lemon (2 to 3 teaspoons)
Pinch of sea salt

If you think eating well means no more deliciously creamy, rich, sweet cheesecake, have I got news for you! And before you panic thinking that a tofu cheesecake couldn't possibly be yummy, I suggest you try this recipe.

Preheat the oven to 350°F and lightly oil a standard pie plate (not deep dish). Finely crumble the graham crackers and mix them with the hempseed and salt. Stir in the water, olive oil, and rice syrup, mixing well to create a stiff crust mixture. Press into the prepared pie plate, covering the bottom and sides evenly. Press foil over the crust to firmly hold it in place. Bake for 12 minutes. Remove the foil and bake 5 minutes longer. Remove from the oven and cool completely.

Place the boiled tofu, rice syrup, olive oil, lemon juice, vanilla extract, and salt in a food processor and purée until smooth and creamy. Spoon evenly into the pie shell and bake 20 to 25 minutes or until the edges are beginning to brown and the center is firm. (Do not bake until the top cracks, as the cheesecake will be dry.) Remove from the oven and cool completely.

For the topping, place the berries, rice syrup, lemon zest, and salt in a saucepan and cook 10 to 12 minutes over low heat until the berries are quite soft and the juices are reduced to a syrup. Spoon the topping evenly over the cooled cheesecake and chill completely to set the topping before slicing.

Variation: You may use fresh berries when they are in season, cooking them in the same manner.

Brownies

Makes about 16 brownies

½ cup light-colored olive oil or avocado oil
½ cup brown rice syrup
1 cup nondairy grain-sweetened chocolate chips
2 teaspoons pure vanilla extract
1 cup whole wheat pastry flour
¼ cup semolina flour
¼ cup coarsely chopped pecans
¼ cup shelled hempseed
1 teaspoon non-aluminum baking powder
Pinch of sea salt
Pinch of ground cinnamon

Try these delicious vegan brownies when you want a homey, comforting dessert. With the nutrient-dense hempseed, you can enjoy them knowing that you're doing something good for your body as well as your chocolate-loving soul.

Preheat the oven to 350°F and lightly oil an 8-inch square baking pan. Combine the olive oil and rice syrup in a small saucepan and place over medium heat. When the mixture foams, remove from the heat and whisk in the chocolate chips and vanilla extract, beating until smooth. Transfer to a mixing bowl and stir in the flours, pecans, hempseed, baking powder, salt, and cinnamon. Bake 30 to 35 minutes or until the edges are firm and the center is soft but not mushy. Remove from the oven and allow to cool completely before slicing into 2-inch squares.

Gingerbread

½ cup barley malt

½ cup brown rice syrup

½ cup light-colored olive oil or avocado oil

1 teaspoon pure vanilla extract

1 teaspoon powdered ginger

1 teaspoon ground cinnamon

Scant pinch of grated nutmeg

Scant pinch of ground cloves

2 cups whole wheat pastry flour

2 teaspoons aluminum-free baking powder

½ teaspoon sea salt

½ to 1 cup vanilla soymilk or rice milk

2 tablespoons shelled hempseed

Preheat the oven to 350°F and lightly oil a 9-inch square baking pan or standard loaf pan.

Whisk together the barley malt, rice syrup, olive oil, and vanilla extract in a large bowl. Whisk in the ginger, cinnamon, nutmeg, and cloves. Gradually stir in the flour, baking powder, and salt. Slowly stir in just enough soymilk to create a smooth batter. Fold in the hempseed. Spoon the batter evenly into the prepared pan and bake 30 to 35 minutes or until the center springs back to the touch.

Variation: For added richness, create a glaze. Combine ½ cup brown rice syrup and 2 teaspoons grated orange zest in a saucepan and heat until foamy. Spoon over the warm or cooled cake.

Sweet and spicy—no, not the perfect date, but the perfect gingerbread! Although if you serve this, your date just might be perfect.

TABLE 1: NUTRITIONAL INFORMATION PER 100 GRAMS
OF VARIOUS PRIMARY HEMPSEED PRODUCTS

	Shelled Hempseed	Whole Hempseed	Hempseed Oil	Hempseed Meal	Hempseed Sprouts
Calories	567	503	730	452	192
Protein	30.6	22.5	0	26.0	10.4
Total Fat	47.2	30.0	81.0	20.0	4.4
Saturated Fat	5.2	3.3	9.0	2.2	n/t
Monounsaturated Fat	5.8	3.7	10.0	2.5	n/t
Polyunsaturated Fat	36.2	23.0	62.0	15.3	n/t
Carbohydrate	10.9	35.8	0	41.0	27.8
Ash	6.6	5.9	n/t	5.5	2.7
Moisture	4.7	5.7	19.0	7.0	54.7
Linoleic acid (LA)	27.6	17.5	57.0	11.7	n/t
Linolenic acid (LNA)	9.2	5.5	19.0	3.7	n/t
Gamma-linolenic acid (GLA)	0.8	0.5	1.7	0.3	n/t
Total Essential Fatty Acids	36.2	23.0	76.0	15.4	n/t
Palmitic acid 16:0	3.4	2.2	4.9	1.5	n/t
Arachidic acid 20:0	0.5	0.2	0.4	0.1	n/t
Oleic acid 18:1	5.8	3.7	12.0	2.5	n/t
Stearic acid 18:0	1.5	0.9	2.1	0.6	n/t
Cholesterol (mg)	0	0	0	0	0
Total Dietary Fiber	6.0	35.1	0	36.5	20.1
Sugars	2.0	n/t	0	5.0	n/t
Vitamin A (B-Carotene) (IU)	231	3.7	19.0	n/t	50.0
Thiamine (Vitamin B_1) (mg)	1.4	0.9	n/t	n/t	0.2
Riboflavin (Vitamin B_2) (mg)	0.3	1.1	n/t	n/t	0.2
Vitamin B_6 (mg)	0.1	0.3	n/t	n/t	0.2
Niacin (Vitamin B_3) (mg)	n/t	2.5	n/t	n/t	n/t
Vitamin C (mg)	1.0	1.4	n/t	n/t	2.0
Vitamin D (IU)	0	10.0	n/t	n/t	1,492.2
Vitamin E (dl-A-tocopherol) (IU)	9.0	3.0	1.0	n/t	4.0
Sodium (mg)	9.0	0	n/t	0	8.9
Calcium (mg)	78.6	1.7	n/t	n/t	176.5
Iron (mg)	9.35	0.2	n/t	n/t	4.8

n/t = not tested   *(Except Calories and as otherwise noted, all units are grams.)*

TABLE 2: AMINO ACID ASSAY PER 100 GRAMS OF HEMPNUT BRAND SHELLED HEMPSEED

Alanine	1.22%
Arginine	3.35%
Aspartic acid	2.97%
Cystine/cysteine	0.39%
Glutamic acid	5.31%
Glycine	1.21%
Histidine*	0.90%
Isoleucine*	1.14%
Leucine*	1.88%
Lysine*	0.91%
Methionine	0.57%
Phenylalanine	1.14%
Proline	1.43%
Serine	1.60%
Threonine*	1.03%
Tryptophan*	0.39%
Tyrosine	1.04%
Valine*	1.42%
Meth+cys*	0.96%
Phen+tyr*	2.19%

*Essential amino acid

Protein Digestibility	0.93
PDCAAS	0.46
PER	1.87

Glossary

Achene: A fruit with a hard shell surrounding it, such as hempseed or almond.

Adherent: The resin that adheres to the outside of the shell of the hempseed. It contains a minute amount of THC, which, if not removed, may end up in a finished product.

Albumin: A simple type of globular protein, the main protein in human blood. Good sources include egg white and hempseed. A very efficient and highly digestible protein and a major source of free radical scavengers.

Bio-remediation: The cultivation of hemp on soils contaminated with heavy metals (near the sites of nuclear accidents) in order to purify the soil and aid in recultivation. Hemp yield and fiber quality are no different from those grown on non-contaminated soils. Hemp removes heavy metals from soils and accumulates them in the roots, seeds, and leaves. Therefore, hempseed from these plants must not be used for any food or animal feed.

Cannabinoid: A class of constituents found only in the resin of the flowering tops of cannabis, including cannabinol (CBN), cannabidiol (CBD), tetrahydrocannabinol (THC), and others. Most are not psychoactive, and some are probably of medicinal value. They have not been adequately researched in the United States because all cannabis, including drug-free industrial hemp, is classified as a Schedule I drug by the DEA, making it unavailable for medical use and research.

Cannabis: A genus of the plant that includes hemp and marijuana. This term refers to the plant itself. Species usually is sativa, and sometimes further mis-classified as *C. indica*, *C. ruderalis*, and others. See also hemp and marijuana.

Cannessence: HempNut, Inc.'s brand of cannabis essential oil, made from hemp or marijuana cultivars. It is derived through a steam-distillate water process that discards nearly all THC. Used for its aromatic components, primarily mono- and sesquiterpene, Cannessence smells sweet and much like cannabis. It has antiviral, antifungal, and antibacterial properties similar to tea tree oil, but with less drying of the skin. It also has aromatherapy properties. A number of body care, perfume, and food products have been produced with this fragrance or flavor.

CBD: Cannabidiol, a cannabinoid found in cannabis. Found more in hemp than marijuana cultivars. Called "anti-THC," as it lodges in the brain's receptor sites, blocking the THC molecule, so no euphoria is caused. Has documented medicinal properties as an analgesic, anti-psychotic, anticonvulsant, anti-inflammatory, and others.

Cultivar: A variety or strain of a plant. There might be as many as ten thousand cultivars of cannabis; the exact number is unknown.

DEA: The U.S. Drug Enforcement Administration. Started by then-President Nixon as a federal police agency controlled by the White House, free of congressional control. Early years often targeted anti-war protesters and political activists. The DEA steadfastly maintains that "hemp is marijuana and marijuana is hemp." Its "Marijuana Eradication Program" of 1998 was directed against industrial hemp—drug-free "ditchweed" that is usually pulled up by local police.

De-fatted hempseed meal: The presscake byproduct of hempseed oil extraction, sometimes called hemp meal or seed cake. Usually contains two-thirds less essential fatty acids than whole hempseed but more protein and fiber. Gluten-free, it has been approved as a safe ingredient by the Celiac Society. Valuable animal feed. Hemp beer brewers use it as flavoring. Popular with manufacturers because of its low cost.

De-hulled hempseed: See shelled hempseed or hulled hempseed.

Edestin: A crystalline globulin protein obtained especially from hempseed, containing all the essential amino acids. From the same Greek root as edible.

Considered a very digestible form of protein. Earlier in the twentieth century it was used in chemistry, science, and animal nutrition and as a general purpose protein.

Essential fatty acids (EFAs): Sometimes called "good fats," these are the two fatty acids that the human body cannot manufacture, so they must come from dietary sources. They are linoleic acid (omega-6, 18:2w6) and alpha-linolenic acid (omega-3, 18:3w3). The 3:1 ratio of omega-6 to omega-3 in hempseed oil is recommended as optimal for long-term health maintenance. EFAs serve as raw materials for cell structure and as precursors for the synthesis of many of the body's biochemicals. Because they are not primarily converted as energy sources, hempseed oil could be considered a "diet" oil. Recommended daily allowance is 2.2 grams of omega-3 and 6.6 grams of omega-6, the amount in 1 tablespoon of hempseed oil or 1 ounce of shelled hempseed. Pregnant and lactating mothers should double their consumption of omega-3.

Fractured hempseed: Whole hempseed that is run through an impact sheller, then packaged and sold without screening or sieving. It is a simple way to comply with USDA requirements regarding sterilization. Innovated by Canadian companies.

Geschält Hanfsamen: Shelled hempseed in German. Usually translated as "peeled hemp seed." See also shelled hempseed.

GLA: Gamma-linolenic acid (GLA, C18:3w6) is derived from the essential fatty acid omega-6. Good sources of GLA include hempseed and hempseed oil (2 to 6 percent GLA in whole hempseed), blue-green algae (spirulina), evening primrose oil, black currant seed oil, borage oil, and some fungal oils. Its alleviating action on psoriasis, atopic eczema, and mastalgia are well researched. GLA has also been under investigation for its beneficial effects on cardiovascular, psychiatric, and immunological disorders.

HACCP: Hazard Analysis and Critical Control Point (pronounced "HAY-sep"). A document, process, and protocol for handling and preparing commercial food. Allows identification of potential hazards and specifies means to prevent the hazard from occurring. Because it will eventually be required of all food producers, the Hemp Food Association (www.HempFood.com) is preparing a suggested HACCP plan for the hempseed food industry.

Hemp: The virtually drug-free version of cannabis. In many countries it is defined as containing less than 0.3 percent THC, the intoxicant found in marijuana. Such a drug model designation reduces technical innovation and allows control of the planting-seed market. Industrial hemp varieties are not capable of intoxication due to the very low THC level and the high level of CBD found in most hemp cultivars. Called *Hanf* in German, *chanvre* in French, *hennep* in Dutch, *cañamo* in Spanish, *canapa* in Italian, *konopi* in Russian, *kannab* in Persian, *kanop* in Armenian, *kanas* in Celtic, *hampa* in Swedish, *kanneh* or *kinnab* in Arabic, *kannabis* in Greek, *cannabis* in Latin, *kannapes* in Lithuanian, *hamppu* in Finnish, *ma* in Mandarin, and *asa* in Japanese.

Hempeh®: HempNut, Inc.'s brand of tempeh, a two thousand-year-old cultured soyfood from Indonesia, to which we add HempNut. It is meaty in taste and appearance and very high in protein, isoflavones, and fiber. Often contains vitamin B_{12}, which is otherwise hard to get in vegan diets.

Hemp flour: A popular but misleading term for de-fatted hempseed meal. Could include flours other than hemp. See also de-fatted hempseed meal.

Hemp grain: A term for technical hempseed, to differentiate from agricultural hemp seed for planting a hemp crop.

Hemp meal: See de-fatted hempseed meal.

Hempnut: A misused term for shelled hempseed. Confusingly similar to HempNut, the brand name invented by the first company, HempNut, Inc., to research, develop, market, and popularize shelled hempseed. The term was recently adopted by many European companies as the German translation

Hanfnüsse, but they have changed the meaning to be whole hempseed, not shelled. See also shelled hempseed and HempNut.

HempNut: The original, trademarked brand of shelled hempseed, invented by Richard Rose.

Hempseed: The seed of the cannabis plant. Actually not a true seed, but an achene, a term for a tiny fruit covered by a hard shell. Called *Hanfsamen* in German, *graine de chanvre* in French, *hennep saat* in Dutch, and *da ma tze* in Chinese. Hempseed is a superior plant food because of its high content of all essential amino acids and the two essential fatty acids, the latter in a ratio required for good human nutrition, and because of its significant content of gamma-linolenic and stearidonic acid.

Hempseed oil: The oil extracted from industrial hempseed. It is an exceptionally rich source of polyunsaturated fatty acids, with uses similar to those of linseed oil. The oil has been used industrially, cosmetically, and nutritionally for many centuries; it served as the first fuel for the diesel engine. However, the nutritional qualities of the oil are particularly important. Available in gel caps or bottles at food stores. The byproduct of hempseed oil manufacture is variously called presscake, seed cake, hemp meal, or de-fatted hempseed meal.

Hempseed protein: Primarily about one-third edestin and two-thirds albumin. A complete protein, it is suitable for animal feed as well as human food. Heat treatment denatures this protein and renders it insoluble, possibly affecting digestibility. A 1998 study suggested that hempseed protein was "most similar to a methionine-rich protein of Brazil nut (*Bertholletia excelsa*) and to Mabinlin IV, a sweetness-inducing protein of *Capparis masaikai*. The high methionine content and the absence of trypsin inhibitory activity suggested that the seed protein can be used to improve the nutritional quality of plant food-stuffs."

HFA: The Hemp Food Association is the only trade group dedicated solely to expanding and enhancing the state of hempseed foods. Members promise to abide by certain quality standards. Founded by author Richard Rose. Has the largest Web site on hempseed and hemp foods: www.HempFood.com.

Hulled hempseed: Same as shelled hempseed. The first English name for it, coined by Richard Rose. Preferred term is now shelled hempseed, as the shell is not a hull; and hulled hempseed can sound confusingly similar to whole hempseed. See also shelled hempseed.

Marijuana: The high-THC version of cannabis, used medicinally and recreationally throughout history. Grown horticulturally with much space around it and bushy like roses, whereas hemp is grown as a crop, closely spaced in rows, like corn, with just a few leaves at the top. Rarely taller than six feet, marijuana looks very different from hemp, which grows as tall as twenty feet.

Omega-3: A category of polyunsaturated fatty acids found in hempseed, including omega-3, SDA, DHA, and EPA. Best sources are hempseed, flaxseed, walnut, and fish oils. The essential fatty acid omega-3 usually accounts for approximately 15 to 25 percent of the total fatty acid content of hempseed.

Omega-6: A category of polyunsaturated fatty acids found in hempseed, including omega-6, GLA, and AA. Good sources include hempseed, flaxseed, canola oil, soybeans, walnuts, and dark green leaves. The essential fatty acid omega-6 accounts for approximately 50 to 70 percent of the total fatty acid content of hempseed.

Omega-9: A category of non-essential monounsaturated fatty acids including oleic acid, which makes up 75 to 80 percent of olive oil.

Organically grown: Grown without the use of synthetic chemicals. Certification must be effected by a third party. Virtually all hempseed is "unsprayed," because it rarely needs herbicides or pesticides. It requires nitrogen for fast growth. The USDA and certain states have laws requiring strict adherence to organic standards by farmers and processors.

Pericarp: The shell of a hempseed.

Peroxide value: A measure of rancidity over time. Varies by product, but high-quality hempseed oil ranges from 0.5 to 5 meq (milli-equivalents). Noticeable rancidity in hempseed oil generally occurs around 7 meq. The EU limit for food oils is 10.

Presscake: The byproduct of hempseed oil manufacture, also called seed cake, hemp meal, or de-fatted hempseed meal. See also de-fatted hempseed meal.

SDA: Stearidonic acid (18:2w3) is derived from the essential fatty acid omega-3. Good amounts are found in hempseed as well as in black currant seed oil. Omega-3 fatty acids are an important factor in the prevention and treatment of cardiovascular as well as inflammatory diseases.

Shell: The hard outer part of the hempseed, composed of the pericarp (the shell) and the testa (the green thin seed membrane between the pericarp and fruit).

Shelled hempseed: Whole hempseed with the hard outer shell removed, leaving only the "fruit." The term was coined and the product innovated by author Richard Rose. Current technology uses an impact sheller and screening process that result in some loss of kernel and admixture of shell fragments. About two and one-half to five pounds of whole hempseed are required to make one pound of shelled hempseed. Also called hulled hempseed or de-hulled hempseed. See also hulled hempseed.

Technical hempseed: Hempseed not for planting (which is "hemp seed") but for manufacturing products such as oil, foods, and varnishes.

Testa: The green inner membrane of a hempseed, separating the kernel (fruit) from the shell (pericarp). Often found in shelled hempseed, as it is difficult to remove.

THC: Delta-9-tetrahydrocannabinol, the euphoriant found in the resin of flowering cannabis. Although the industrial hemp plant is very low in THC, the resin sometimes sticks to the outside of the seed's shell. If the seed is not shelled or cleaned properly, very small amounts of THC may be found in the finished products, sometimes creating a "positive" for marijuana in drug tests. Most governments require hemp to contain less than 0.3 percent THC.

USDA: The U.S. agency with true jurisdiction over industrial hemp growing, although, years ago, the DEA exerted its authority over hemp farming (authority can be transferred from one agency to another only after public hearings, which were not held). To stop "noxious weeds," including hemp, from growing and proliferating, the USDA requires whole hempseed to be sterilized.

Viable hempseed: Hempseed which, if planted, will grow (not merely sprout) to become a plant. In the United States, whole hempseed is required to be nonviable through sterilization. Apart from just shelling the seed, sterilization can be effected through the use of heat (steam or dry heat at 212°F for fifteen minutes), radiation, or fracturing. It must be performed in a facility certified by the USDA.

Whole hempseed: Hempseed with an intact shell. It is not a true seed but an achene, a tiny fruit covered by a hard shell. Whole hempseed contains approximately 20 to 25 percent protein, 20 to 30 percent carbohydrates, 25 to 35 percent oil, and 10 to 15 percent insoluble fiber, as well as a rich array of minerals, particularly phosphorous, potassium, magnesium, sulfur, and calcium, along with modest amounts of iron and zinc. It is also a fair source of carotene, a Vitamin A precursor, and a potentially important contributor of dietary fiber. Shelling increases nutritional content (except fiber) by approximately 40 percent. In Traditional Chinese Medicine, whole hempseed is believed to act on the spleen, stomach, and large intestine meridians and to relieve constipation. Indications include blood deficiency and deficiency of body fluid.

Zero THC: If a hemp product contains no detectable THC according to U.S. Custom's testing methods USCL Method F0-03, it is considered to be "zero THC," "no THC," "THC-free," or "DEA exempt."

about the authors

Richard Rose is founder, president, and "Chief Hemp Nut" of HempNut, Inc., a food company specializing in researching, developing, and marketing hempseed foods, the first two of which were introduced in 1994. He is also founder and president of Omega Nova Corporation, specializing in novel omega-3 delivery systems, and until its sale in 2001 was founder and president of Rella Good Cheese Company (formerly known as Sharon's Finest), a food product development and marketing firm making many cheese alternatives, including TofuRella®. In 1998, Richard founded the Hemp Food Association, dedicated to improving the quality of education, production, and marketing of hempseed foods.

Cooking since childhood, he has been making and marketing natural foods commercially since 1979. In the 1980s Richard invented and marketed more than sixty new products based on tofu and soymilk (under the Brightsong Tofu brand), and his was the only small or natural food company to be named one of the "Top Ten Innovators of 1985" by *Food and Beverage Marketing* magazine. In 1981 he opened and ran one of the first 100-percent nondairy vegetarian restaurants (so long ago the word "vegan" hadn't yet been popularized), using only foods made with tofu and other soy products.

In 1986, the company's main product, TofuRella®, was introduced, sales of which landed the firm on the *Inc.* 500 list of fastest growing companies in the U.S. in 1993 (950 percent growth in five years). The cheese alternative is still sold today in supermarkets and natural food stores in the U.S., Canada, and Europe. The firm helped pioneer the concept of vegetarian foods merchandised in produce sections, a now-common practice.

Born in 1956, Richard has long put his beliefs "where his mouth is," literally: a vegetarian since age twelve and still a vegan since age twenty-two, his personal mission is to introduce and popularize the use of super-nutritious hempseed for food, in order to reduce the deleterious health and planetary effects of the animal-based diet. Richard started HempNut, Inc. in order to develop and market new hempseed foods, starting with HempRella® cheese alternative and Hempeh® Burgers, both introduced in 1994. He also invented and marketed HempNut® brand shelled hempseed, peanut butter, hempseed oil, whole food bars, chocolate chip cookies, organic blue corn chips, HempScream®, and lip balm.

Richard was awarded the 1997 Hemp Times "Bioneer Award" for Outstanding Achievement in Food, the 1997 Hemp World "Hempy Award" for Food, and the 1998 Hemp World "Hempy Award" for Product Innovation for his HempNut® brand of shelled hempseed. He has received a Citizen Citation from Mayor Kurt Schmoke of Baltimore, Maryland, for his work with hempseed foods. The acknowledged father of the U.S. hemp foods movement, Richard is directly responsible for the use of hempseed in over thirty-five hemp industry dinners, and many new companies have adopted his vision of a hemp foods future.

Richard has appeared on hundreds of radio shows, dozens of TV shows, including a nine-minute segment on hemp foods on the CBS-TV national program *The Roseanne Show*, and has been the subject of hundreds of newspaper and magazine stories.

Richard may be reached at P.O. Box 2036, Sebastopol, California, 95473-2036, USA, or by email at hello@richardrose.com.

Christina Pirello is the Emmy Award® winning host of the television series *Christina Cooks*, which airs on more than 135 public television stations nationwide, 50 countries internationally, through the Discovery Health Network, and on Comcast's CN8 Network. She is a bright, free-spirited, vivacious redhead who found her way to Philadelphia by opening a map and dropping a pin.

Her relationship with food began at young age, cooking with her mother and then later, while living in Florida, working as a caterer and pastry chef. But the real pivotal point in her life came at age twenty-six, when after being diagnosed with terminal leukemia, she decided to forgo conventional medical therapies and turned to a nutritional approach—whole foods—and cured herself. This passion and commitment is what makes her so wonderfully inspirational at what she does.

For the last sixteen years, Christina has been teaching whole foods cooking classes, and conducting lifestyle seminars and lecturing on the power of food in our lives, nationwide in a variety of settings from natural food stores to corporate boardrooms to network television.

Since 1989, she and her husband have been publishing a bi-monthly whole foods magazine, *Christina Cooks*, with national distribution and circulation, as well as operating Christina Trips, a travel company that specializes in healthy vacations to exotic destinations. The author of the best-selling cookbook, *Cooking the Whole Foods Way*, Christina has released her second and third books, *Cook Your Way to the Life You Want*, and *Glow, A Prescription for Radiant Health and Beauty*, and has published her fourth book, *Christina Cooks:*

Everything You Always Wanted to Know About Whole Foods, but Were Afraid to Ask, in January 2004.

Christina won an Emmy Award in the category of Best Host and is beginning the sixth season of her PBS series. She is featured consistently in newspapers and national magazines, as well as on television and radio. In addition, she is on the faculty of Drexel University. She also serves as chairman of the Philadelphia chapter of Chefs Collaborative, a culinary organization dedicated to the creation of sustainable agriculture and preservation of the quality of our food supply, and is a member of the Fair Food Project, IACP (International Association of Culinary Professionals), and Women Chefs and Restaurateurs.

Brigitte Mars is an herbalist and nutritional consultant from Boulder, Colorado, who has been working with natural medicine for mor than thirty years. She teaches herbology through Esalen, Boulder College of Massage Therapy, and Naropa University.

A professional member of the American Herbalists Guild, Brigitte is the author of *Sex, Love and Health*, *Addiction Free Naturally*, and *Rawsome!* She is proud to educate people on the many benefits of hemp.

Brigitte's Web site is www.brigittemars.com.

Links, Bibliography, and Resources

For more information on Richard Rose: www.TheHempNut.com
  (For an extensive bibliography on hempseed-related information, please go to the listing for *The HempNut Cookbook* on the publisher's website: www.bookpubco.com)
Brigitte Mars: www.brigittemars.com
Christina Pirello: www.christinacooks.com
Dr. Dave West, botanist: www.industrialhemp.net
The Drug Library, extensive hemp section: www.druglibrary.org
French Meadow Bakery: www.frenchmeadow.com
Global Hemp: www.globalhemp.com
Health Canada, search for hemp regulations: www.hc-sc.gc.ca

Recipes Using Hempseed and Hemp Oil

recipes using hempseed

recipes using hempseed oil

Index

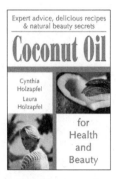
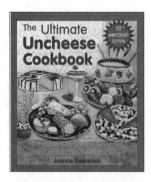

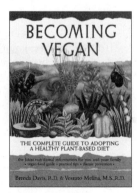